# CALCULATED FUTURES

# CALCULATED FUTURES

## Theology, Ethics, and Economics

D. Stephen Long
Nancy Ruth Fox
with Tripp York

BAYLOR UNIVERSITY PRESS

*Cover Design* by Pamela Poll
The following are reprinted and used by permission of the publishers.
Chap. 1: "Profits and Prophets: Theology and Economics in Conflict?" with
Nancy Fox in Edward O'Boyle, ed., *Teaching the Social Way of Thinking* (Edwin
Mellon Press, 1999)
Chap. 2: "What Make Theology Political: Come Let Us Reason Together," in
*Political Theology* 5, no. 4 (October 2004). Used by permission of Equinox
Publishing, London.
Chap. 4: "The Theology of Economics: Adam Smith as 'Church' Father," *The
Other Journal*, issue 5: *Capitalism*, 2005.
Chap. 5: "Corporations and the Common Good" in *Ave Maria Law Review* 4,
no. 1.
Chap. 7: "Catholic Social Teaching and the Global Market," in Doug Bandow
and David Schindler, eds., *Wealth Poverty and Human Destiny* (Wilmington,
Delaware: ISI Books, 2003).
Chap. 8: "Offering our Gifts: The Politics of Remembrance," with Tripp York in
Stanley Hauerwas and Samuel Wells, eds., *Blackwell Companion to Christian
Ethics* (Blackwell, 2004).

Library of Congress Cataloging-in-Publication Data

Long, D. Stephen, 1960-
 A calculated future : theology, ethics, and the politics of faith / D. Stephen
Long, Nancy Ruth Fox ; with Tripp York.
   p. cm.
 ISBN 978-1-60258-014-5 (alk. paper)
 1. Economics–Religious aspects–Christianity. 2. Christianity and politics. 3.
Ethics. I. Fox, Nancy Ruth. II. York, Tripp. III. Title.

 BR115.E3L655 2007
 261.8'5–dc22

                              2007026449

# CONTENTS

PART II

The Corporation and Everyday Economic Life:
A Traditioned Theological Inquiry

# INTRODUCTION

Many of us watched in 1989 when the Berlin wall fell, and with it the cold war ended. It could have heralded the dawn of a new day in which old, tired arguments between the so-called political left and right were likewise dismantled. That did not happen. Some on the political right quickly proclaimed victory, even viewing that day as apocalyptic. We had come to the "end of history" where western style liberalism was now our only future. "We are all capitalists now," suggested Michael Novak, "even the pope." Some theologians who had once been committed to a socialist vision now changed course, heralding globalization as the new form Christian mission must take if we are truly concerned for the poor and committed to social justice. Even those on the left were affected by these changes. Latin American liberation theology with its commitment to dependency theory changed its tune. But the tired conversation between the political left and the right and its ecclesial counterparts, the "progressives" and "traditionalists," remains unabated, with only a few new variations.

The "progressives" turned their focus from economic structures to questions of sex and gender. "Progressive" Christianity seems preoccupied with securing rights to abortion and sexual expression as the issues of "social justice" before us. Little nuance occurs in these arguments, and little self-criticism exists that would begin to ask why it is that these issues are central to late-modern, late-capitalist western European citizens in a way that they are not to the rest of the world, especially to global Christianity. The "leftist" or progressive Christian movement continues to support "liberation" from tyranny and to overuse terms like hegemonic and empire until they become clichés. Of course, this movement often also seeks to liberate us from every kind of doctrinal or moral accountability the church traditionally taught. For this reason, no one should fear this movement. It will not sustain itself within the life of the church. There can be no leftist Christian vision when there is nothing left of the Christian vision.

Yet little comfort can be found among those on the right who originally reacted against the dominance of the leftist or progressive Christian vision among the Protestant Church's hierarchy. If the 'Christian leftist vision' has refused self-criticism and adopted a liberal bourgeois agenda embracing promiscuity under the guise of "social justice," the "Christian neoconservative vision" has done no better. Its embrace of the corporation and free-market economics before and after 1989 proved to be as failed a historical project as the uncritical acceptance of the socialist and communist vision by the left. Convinced that the materialism of communism represented the true threat to faith, it looked the other way when confronted with the overturning of Christian tradition in free market economics. We now know the result: Enron, Tyco, Worldcom, Arthur Andersen. . . . The ties among these corporate fiascos, their devastating consequences on peoples' lives, and the church should cause us to take stock and ask what went wrong, but no such self-searching seems to take place on the Christian right. These are all just exceptions to the otherwise easy compatibility between Christianity and global capitalism. The Christian right consistently ignores the "logic" to the global, free market that runs as counter to the Christian gospel as the "logic" of materialism on the political left. Both end in nihilism and both are species of that programmatic atheism that defines western secularity, even when it still allows space for God as a private, consumer option. The church has uncritically invited this logic of the free market into its own house through the thoroughgoing utilitarianism of the "church growth movement" and the uncritical adoption of management theory through a preoccupation with "leadership." We treat people like consumers, speak about "target audiences of the unchurched" and sell the gospel through means that cannot be differentiated from how any other commodity is sold in the marketplace.

A Different Theological Economics: The Church as Transnational

Is a different kind of theological economics possible, one that will not get mired in these tired debates? Rather than rehearsing the well-known and predictable arguments among these two aging movements, Christians can find a different kind of argument about theological economics by beginning with the orthodox confession that the church is one, holy, catholic and apostolic; for this simple confession contains in seed an intriguing and inescapable vision of a theological economics. Central to Jesus' mission is the gathering of the twelve and establishing them, through the Holy Spirit at Pentecost, as a new global political reality, which we know as the church. This community is constituted through Christ's body, which is raised and now mediated to the church through Word and sacrament. It participates in his glorious reign through his Ascension. As the body of Christ in the world, the church is a transnational, global community whose allegiance takes priority over all other allegiances—especially those of the nation-state and the corporation. This allegiance requires a faithful, disciplined life in both our politics and economics. It assumes at the very least a commitment to refuse to kill other Christians in the name of the nation-state or the free market. And it requires a disciplined use of economic resources such that communal forms of sharing will take precedence over individual rights to hold private property, as Acts 2 and 4 teach us. This disciplined economic life will also require a reaffirmation of disciplined sexual activity, for much of the conversation about sexuality today is really a veiled discussion of economics. If we are free to exchange bodily fluids without any communal accountability, then we will preserve the freedom to exchange other commodities based on our preferences alone.[1] This does not, of course, tell us exactly how exchanges should take place. Nor does it call us to withdraw from every form of the modern corporation. Even if that were possible, which it is not, it would not be proper. Every corporation is not equal to Enron, Worldcom and Tyco. In fact, I hope to provide evidence of other kinds of corporations that are much more fitting with the Christian life in the essays that follow. I want to think reasonably and practically about what faithful exchanges look like within the orthodox confession that we believe in the one, holy, catholic and apostolic church.

To think of economics within the confession of the catholic church is not to replace the market or economics with the church or theology. Obviously, the church cannot accomplish, and should not try to, all that the market does. It cannot efficiently collect garbage, recycle, provide clean water nor provide many of the basic goods that make daily life possible. To argue that the church is an alternative economy to the capitalist one is to use the term *economy* analogically. The divine economy and the market economy do not use the term identically, nor do they use it equivocally. This creates confusion, as the dialogue in this work between the economist Nancy Fox and myself, as a theologian, demonstrates. It also creates confusion among theologians.

In her *Economy of Grace*, Kathryn Tanner rightly argues against thinking that Christianity might be "thrown entirely on its own resources to generate, apart from the workings of the present system, a viable economic alternative" (Tanner, 2005, 88). She writes,

> With nothing to gain from attention to the capitalist system it hopes to escape, theological economy might limit its purview to the Bible or to church practices, and model its self-reliant, small-scale communities on, say, the subsistence agrarian economies of ancient Israel or on the desert monasteries of the early church, withdrawn from a world in which hope has been lost. Pretending to self-sufficiency, an alternative theological economy might in this way cut itself off from any sophisticated economic analysis of the realities of today's world – a sophisticated analysis of the real problems and potentials for change in the economic situation we now face, as the best academic disciplines of the day describe them. (Tanner, 2005, 88)

Tanner's concern seems to be fourfold. First, this version of a theological economy will be sectarian and limit its development only to the Bible or church practices. Second, in so doing, it will be self-deceived by pretending that these sources alone can generate a theological economics without attention to real everyday economic exchanges. We will not be able to recognize the true conditions of our daily existence. Third, such a strategy is a counsel of despair that withdraws from the world for it views capitalism as so thoroughly ungodly it loses hope that it offers us anything with which to work. It invites Christians to flee to the desert. Fourth, this counsel of despair neglects the difficult task of a charitable and generous engagement with the best rationality present in the social sciences.

I agree with her, and if I do not always take this into account in the following work it is because I do not think it is possible to create some desert space where we can withdraw and create an economic alternative based solely on some pure Christianity.

This is no threat anyone should fear. If anyone were tempted to think that a sectarian Christian economy could be produced separate from the real, everyday economic exchanges that already constitute our lives, he would be mistaken. Christians should cultivate a distinct way of life, and movements such as the New Monasticism emerging in some quarters of the church are intriguing and ought to be encouraged (Byasse, 2005). Nevertheless, they are no flight to the desert; no such place exists.

Although it is impossible to think or act in some alternative Christian economy separate from the everyday exchanges global capitalism makes possible, it is possible to think or act in those everyday exchanges and not recognize they always bring with them theological convictions. This is the real sectarian option—to think some pure social and economic space exists for analysis free from theology. Theology and social analysis are always already linked. When we are doing theology we are already doing political and economic analysis. When economists are doing economics they are also doing theology. The question is which theology is being done, not if it is being done. Everything is theological.[2]

That everything is theological does not mean God should be used to legitimate or explain everything else. I once taught theology at a Catholic university where nearly all my students had gone through a Catholic secondary education. They now found themselves, once again, in a mandatory theology course, and many of them did not want to be there. I began an opening lecture on the Trinity one semester when a clearly agitated business major threw up his hand and blurted, "How is this course going to help me market a taco?" It was just the right question; for it gave an opportunity to explain the ancient sacred wisdom that the knowledge of God is an end it itself; it is never to be used for something else. It should not be politicized; it cannot, and should not, be turned into some paradigm that must demonstrate its usefulness in some political sphere. We worship God because it is true and good to do so, not because it is useful. As St. Augustine rightly taught us, God is to be enjoyed, not used. Every other created thing is to be used to assist us in that enjoyment. We cannot think about a Christian politics or economics without recognizing this claim. The doctrine of the Trinity is not useful for politics; it is true. To use God for political or economic ends is to take God's name in vain. That everything is theological then means something different from this; it means that everything which is creature, by virtue of being creature, bears some sign, some mark, some relation to the Creator, and theologians must narrate all those creatures within the divine economy. The market is not an atheological reality; it is a creature. As such it bears theological significance.

Buying the Future: What Credit is That to You?

That economics is theological can be shown in the very language we use to speak about it—debt, gift, redemption, credit, fiduciary, exchange. How do these terms relate to the divine economy? Which "economy" renders them intelligible? Whether we should use these terms within the divine economy at all is a matter of debate and an important one. It begins the process of thinking about economics within the divine economy. For instance, Oliver O'Donovan finds the term *exchange* to be inappropriate as does Kathryn Tanner the language of debt and obligation.

O'Donovan writes, "'Exchange' imports the idea of closure to a transaction, restoring the parties to the independence of the status quo ante, each strengthened by the return of value in a different form" (O'Donovan, 2005, 246). He reads the term exchange primarily in the context of a contract and denies the possibility of its usefulness in terms of the language of gift. He rightly cautions against any such contractual use of exchange in theology, "The concept of exchange is not fundamental to community. It is a device, abstract and formal, created together with the institution of trade, the market. To trade is to effect an exchange of goods between two otherwise equal and unrelated agents" (O'Donovan, 2005, 246).

O'Donovan places the term *communication* (from *koinonia*) as a theological term more basic than exchange. He quotes Althusius who defines communcation as goods held in common such as "things, services, and common rights (*iura*), by which the numerous and various needs of each and every symbioate are supplied, the self-sufficiency and mutuality of life and human society are achieved, and social life is established and conserved." To communicate is to give anything "meaning" and thus has as its "paradigm object" the word (O'Donovan, 2005, 250). O'Donovan's replacement of the term exchange with communication helps us avoid thinking of exchanges in terms of contracts that mediate between strangers, who then remain distant from one another rather than being in communion with each other. His counsel is wise, although I'm not convinced that the terms themselves —*exchange* versus *communion*—can bear alone the significance he seems to give them. Exchange is a translation of *mutare*, which can also mean mutuality and reciprocity. Althusius assumes such in his definition when he explains communication as "mutuality of life."

Kathryn Tanner also expresses concerns with contractual language being written into the divine economy, but for a different reason. O'Donovan does so for the purposes of "communion;" Tanner does so for the sake of a disinterested grace. She writes, "Notions of debt, contractual obligation, loan, even stewardship should be written out of the Christian story about God's relations to the world and our relations with God and one another, in light of an understanding of grace that is incompatible with them" (Tanner, 2005, 56). This is because grace is disinterested. For Tanner, the gift of grace "comes with no strings attached," for "giving is completely disinterested without self-concern, solely for the well-being or pleasure of others" (Tanner, 2005, 57).

Inasmuch as terms such as debt and obligation imply a restricted economy where everything is reduced to a contractual relation, we should also heed Tanner's counsel. Yet most of us have contracts with our employers, for which we are grateful, and it is appropriate to ask why. We also have loans and debts that make possible college educations, homes and many other necessities of everyday life. Indeed others don't have access to these things and that is an injustice we should seek to remedy. Nevertheless, this should not prevent us from being thankful for them or hoping and working for the time when others do have them. These things for which we are grateful are indeed based on mutual obligations that allow us to communicate with others. In fact, the gifts we give our spouses, children, friends, and others do have certain expectations and obligations; they are forms of 'communication' that implicate our lives together into a common life of mutual sharing and obligation. We do not give ourselves to one another solely for the sake of the well-being or pleasure of the other such that we would intentionally sacrifice our own well-being or pleasure for the sake of the other. Martyrdom should always come as an unintended "gift."

Tanner's doctrine of a disinterested grace has ecclesial and liturgical significance as well as economic. She writes "in praise of open communion" (Tanner, 2004, 473–85). The debate over "open communion" in Protestant churches is, like our debates over sex, a debate about economics. A theological defense that separates the Eucharist from baptism and views the Eucharist primarily as a form of hospitality that is open to all without the prerequisite of baptismal vows fits well with a notion of disinterested grace. But is it any more plausible in everyday church life than an economy of grace is possible given the actual exchanges within which we must live everyday? Take away those vows, take away the "exodus" that initiates the Christian life by journeying out into the desert, and the sustaining presence of the Eucharist will be given a new significance that ruptures our practice with that which went before. It will no longer make sense in terms of the story of Israel where the Eucharist is a calling grounded in a covenant with mutual obligations. If grace is disinterested, no such mutual obligation is possible.

O'Donovan and Tanner instruct us on being careful as to the economic language we use in doing theology. They also show us that it matters for how we think about the politics of the church's life. We also find resources for thinking about the analogical relationship between the divine economy and market economics outside of

Christian theology. They can be found in contemporary philosophical discussions on metaphysics. For instance, Philip Goodchild suggests, "There is but a single ontological problem: 'What is money?'" (Goodchild, 2005, 130). This "single ontological problem" emerges from his recognition of an "extraordinary paradox," which is, "the practice of critique is informed by ontology, while ontology is informed by the practice of critique. And the persistent question emerges: can the Real, even within capitalism, be exhausted by practice, by what happens, by temporal and social relations" (Goodchild, 2005, 129). Any analysis of money only indebted to assessing temporal, social relations neglects this ontological question. Money is much more than what it is at any moment.

Money is a financial instrument. In his basic introduction to neoliberal economics, Charles Wheelan identifies "four simple" uses for financial instruments. First they raise capital by allowing us to borrow money; they make possible "credit" (Wheelan, 2002, 120). We borrow money we do not have today in hope and anticipation of what we will have in the future. Second, money "stores, protects and makes profitable use of excess capital." It does this by establishing a "rental rate" for capital –r– the rate of interest (Wheelan, 2002, 121). Third, money functions as insurance against risk by futures buying (Wheelan, 2002, 123). Finally, money also makes possible "speculation" through futures buying. It can be used to insure risk or to take risk.[3] Money buys a possible future through making credit, interest, insurance and speculation possible.

Because money is credit, interest, insurance and speculation, it is not something "real" to which we can point. Money is virtuality. Therefore it will require a different kind of analysis than a Marxist praxis based critique. It will require one that opens up to questions of metaphysics, religion and theology in a way Marxism can never adequately entertain. Financial instruments trust in a future that might be, in a future that is not yet, but is only promised. They are forms of belief. In buying credit, I am buying a future.[4] I am making an eschatological gesture. For this reason Goodchild makes the important and somewhat startling claim, "if credit may lead to creation, then, in a reversal of ideology critique, *what we are may be determined more fundamentally by what we believe than what we do*" (Goodchild, 2005, 143) If Goodchild is correct, then belief matters more than we assume in contemporary theology. It too is a matter of credit; it imagines a future we do not yet know and through that imagination opens up the possibility not so much of buying a potenital future as a pure essence and making it real, but participating in one that we take on credit God has prepared, and is preparing, for us.

That financial instruments are forms of belief in a future—in credit and interest—should not surprise theologians. Jesus also taught this and this teaching has been received throughout the tradition in anticipation of the future he inaugurated but did not yet complete.

In Christian theology Jesus is the future, he is the anticipation of an end given in the middle whose risen body funds an economy both present and future. As William Cavanaugh has argued, the body of Christ given to us through the Eucharist mediates an account of being where each "fraction" of the Eucharistic element is the fullness of Christ's body (Cavanaugh, 1999, 190). This too is a form of credit; Jesus is the object of belief in both a real presence and, through his absence, an imagined future. For this reason we can never have a secure ecclesial politics of identity for Jesus always stands over and against the church, which gathers in hope and trust that he will come even when he is not here. He stands as a funding source for what is present and yet at the same time he is absent. As Rowan Williams notes, the fact that our churches are signs devoid of Christ prevents any fetishization of his presence. The empty tomb tradition "is, theologically speaking, part of the church's resource in resisting the temptation to 'absorb' Jesus into itself, and thus part of what its confession of the divinity of Jesus amounts to in spiritual and political practice" (Williams, 1999, 192). This spiritual and political practice poses a question that always stands in judgment over and against us—"what credit is that to you?"

The fact that our churches are empty tombs devoid of Jesus' presence should not alarm us. Instead it produces a desire that avoids fetishization for the desire flourishes in the absence of any specific 'commodity.' On the one hand this desire cannot be satisfied, Jesus is not here. But on the other, the absence of Jesus as object does not produce violence because the One for whom we wait appears in Word and sacrament. Even while absent; his material body is now inexhaustible.

### THEOLOGICAL ECONOMICS AS HOLINESS

Rather than engaging in debates over whether Christianity should be in service to capitalism or socialism, theological economics would benefit by remembering that most of the church's economic analysis took place within the context of the call to holiness. This is no retreat from social and political matters, this call is what made these issues social and why the church must address them. Jesus' material presence sanctifies the world by fulfilling the Law, but his absence makes space for an ongoing performance of his completion of the Law that completes it yet more. Sometimes he fulfills the Law by diminishing its letter for the sake of its spirit. He plucks grain and heals on the Sabbath. Sometimes he fulfills it by strengthening its letter for the sake of its spirit. He strengthens the prohibition against divorce, against taking another's life and against loaning money at interest. He receives the teaching of Moses and brings it to completion by disclosing its spirit; for Jesus is the Torah of God, the Word made flesh or the Eternal Wisdom made manifest in human form. His very Person fulfills the Law, uniting what is bodily and composite with divine simplicity. His body itself is the physical letter of the Law united with true Spirit. For this reason, the more we hear and obey the letter the more we find it "porous," opening us to its mysterious spirit whether it comes to us through allegory, anagogy or tropology. The letter and the spirit of the Law are not to be reduced to each other; their distinct natures remain. But in the Person of Christ they are One. The letter of the Law then does not close us within an immanence of being, but opens us up to its mystery. It gives the letter an inexhaustible depth making it always contemporary. Jesus is always fulfilling the Law, showing us new dimensions to it and mediating new practices for us to embody and for which we wait. Each reception of Jesus' completion of the Law completes it yet more. This is the church's mission, its task is to sanctify God's creation.

Jesus strengthens the prohibition against certain forms of credit and interest by telling us:

> If you love those who love you, what credit is that to you? For even sinners love those who love them. If you do good to those who do good to you, what credit is that to you? For even sinners do the same. If you lend to those from whom you hope to receive, what credit is that to you? Even sinners lend to sinners, to receive as much again. But love your enemies, do good and lend, expecting nothing in return. Your reward will be great and you will be children of the Most High; for he is kind to the ungrateful and the wicked. Be merciful, just as your Father is merciful. (Luke 6:32-36, NRSV)

Jesus raises the metaphysical question of credit and interest and poses a question of his own—"what credit is that to you?"[5] His response to this metaphysical question is complex. He correlates taking interest on money with ontology, ethics and theology. Loans and the expectations we have of them signify what we will be, as well as how our being relates to the good and to the Blessed Trinity. Jesus does not teach a disinterested ethic here. This is not proto-kantianism. We should lend such that we expect a "reward." But nor is this Adam Smith's butcher, brewer and baker who looks only to her own interest and thereby serves the common good through unintended consequences. Interest for Jesus is a much more complex matter than that. The Trinity is not some Stoic providence that ensures harmony out of conflict. This is not the credit that imagines a blessed future. Of course we have a self-interest, a *conatus essendi* that is a necessary feature of theology, ethics and ontology. This desire to be requires living out of credit for none of us can sustain his or her own life. Projects of an immanent sustainability often entail reproductive regulations and forced relocations that make Malthus look moderate. Instead of such an immanent and inevitably violent sustainability, we are to lend without expectation of return from those to whom we lend, but lend with an expectation of return from God. Why? Because this is how God sanctifies the creation.

This is a mission Christians share with Jews and Muslims, albeit with significant differences in practice, which requires each of us to examine seriously the exchanges involved in lending and borrowing. Meir Tamari reminds us that the reason for the interest prohibition in the Torah is because, "in the words of the *Sefer Hachinuch*, [God] wanted to purify the Jew so that he should go beyond the normal actions" (Tamari, 1991, 106). We glimpse this same quest for holiness in the past and future enactments of Jesus' twist to the ontological problem "what is money?" He does not resolve the problem for all places and all times, but turns the question against us, "what credit is that to you?" Does your credit have place for God as the One who rewards? Does it go beyond what is expected of "sinners"?

How can this be something more than pious nonsense? What kind of reward are we to expect from God? Is this another version of "cartoon Platonism" where we forego rewards here for the sake of a univocal yet intensified reward in the hereafter? It can only avoid this if we understand the mediation of God's reward ecclesiologically. This too is part of Jesus' teaching on money. After the rich young ruler is turned away, Jesus' disciples ask him whether anyone can be saved. Peter reminds him that they left everything to follow him. Jesus does not respond that self-sacrifice is its own reward. He does not tell Peter that in giving a gift without any possible return he has given the only possible gift. Instead he says, "Truly I tell you, there is no one who has left house or wife or brothers or parents or children, for the sake of the kingdom of God, who will not get back very much more in this age, and in the age to come eternal life" (Lk. 18: 29-30). That is not cartoon Platonism; it is a promissory note, a kind of credit that exceeds the credit capitalism promises. It is the credit out of which the church must live even when it only glimpses its existence in the Blessed Sacrament.

For this to be more than pious nonsense, we must imagine transnational religious identities where "economic interest" exceeds individual preferences grounded in freedom as self-assertion. We do not need to invent this economy de novo. Instead, we find resources for it in the Christian tradition and in a similar sensibility in both Islam and Judaism as they have received the teaching from Moses, the prophet and Jesus on money. For despite our differences, we share a similar task, which is to sanctify rather than instrumentalize the world. This similar task now stands against a western secular program that postulates a different mediation of being than do our religious traditions. This other ontology arrives with something like Jeremy Bentham's "Defense of Usury," where he wrote, "no man of ripe years, and of sound mind, ought out of lovingkindness to him, to be hindered from making such a bargain, in the way of obtaining money, as, acting with his eyes open, he deems conducive to his interest" (Bentham, 1952, 163). This is a way of being that only knows interest. The difference between the secular rise of modern ethics after Bentham, and Christian (as well as Islamic and Jewish) reflection on economics prior to Bentham, involves a complete break in how one thinks about money. Make no mistake, capitalism can never have an understanding of liberty that is something other than Bentham's. To embrace capitalism is to embrace this liberal ontology and for that reason Christianity can never finally embrace capitalism. That Christianity can never embrace capitalism is readily found throughout the tradition when it receives Jesus' teaching on credit and interest.

How might we move the conversation about theology and economics beyond the tired shibboleths of the Christian 'left' and 'right?' We can begin by being attentive to the language we use in our everyday economic exchanges and relating it to the language we use in Christian doctrine. Placing that language within the context of the church's common (and therefore social) pursuit of holiness will also prove illuminating.

I do not write for economists, but for people in the church; some of whom are economists, many of whom own or work in business every day. I want to remind them of the church's traditional teachings on economics and see what bearing they have on everyday life. The point is to consider what a faithful form of "exchange" would envision. I am a theologian and not an economist and therefore I confess that I have no idea how to build a global economic system. I have no expectation that my work will somehow lead to the overthrow of the IMF or the WTO; and I certainly do not seek the implementation of some theocratic regime that will once again refuse to lend money at interest through a coercive will to power. Although I do think Christians should be attentive to the alternative forms of banking Islam is producing, my concerns are more modest. How might we help the faithful embody the virtues of the Christian life and avoid its vices? What difference do our doctrines make for how we think through the first principles of economic exchange? Such questions may have revolutionary or reformist implications, but overthrowing, legitimating, or reforming a global economic system is not my primary concern. This does not mean indifference to the plight of those who unjustly suffer under various economic regimes; justice is one of the virtues we must embody.

The following essays are an effort to address two questions in an attempt to develop a *Christian* vision of a common economic life. (1) How can we best embody the Christian virtues and avoid deadly vices given the economy within which we must live? (2) What difference do our Christian doctrines make for how we should think about economic exchanges?

My life has been greatly enriched by persons who do embody economic practices out of the mainstream like Reba Place and The Church of the Servant King; both seek first to be faithful and, yet, operate businesses that remain fiscally viable. I do not think they fled to the desert, but they certainly produced interesting communal businesses that appear to challenge Smithian orthodoxy in favor of a more Christian orthodoxy. I do not think that the onus has to be on them to justify how they are not sectarian because they operate outside the orthodox wisdom of the science of economics. I think we can learn as much from such communities as we can by engaging with the best in the academic discipline of economics, but surely this is not an either-or. We can do both.

I do not think the development of a Christian vision can take place in isolation from other religious traditions or secular politics. This is why the first two essays in this collection occur between a Jewish economist and myself as a theologian. "Prophets and Profits" and "The Facts about Values," are an attempt at a serious engagement between the disciplines of theology and economics. These two essays developed out of work that Nancy Fox, associate professor of economics at Saint Joseph's University, and I did together. We had the delightful task of teaching an interdisciplinary honors course in theology and economics. This was not a course in business ethics, because it did not assume compatibility between theology and economics; this was precisely what was explored—the logic of both disciplines. How can theology and economics be brought into conversation? Where are the commonalties? Where are the differences? Are the differences incommensurable? What role should the church's social teachings have in economics? Does the market intrude into ecclesial life? The irony that a Methodist theologian and a Jewish economist should be called upon at a Jesuit Catholic institution to teach primarily Italian and Irish Catholic students about the heritage of Catholic social teaching should not be lost on our readers.

Our interdisciplinary course sought to avoid positioning theology and economics in terms of any *a priori* structure. We did assume that if God can be found in all things, as the Jesuits teach, then economics and theology should be integrated more fully than the fact/value distinction, or the normative/positive economic distinction permits. Yet, if this is to result in something more than a mere pious platitude, a serious encounter between theology and economics is necessary. Because we sought this serious encounter, we began and concluded the course recognizing an uncertainty as to the relationship between theology and economics. As the scholastics taught us, we divided in order to unite. We were, however, better at dividing than uniting. Even in this work, I leave it to the reader to do the work of integration.

Because our goal was to investigate the differences and similarities between economics and theology, it already assumed the inadequacy of merely tolerating economics as an autonomous social science or theology as supernatural excursions into some ineffable spiritual realm of "value." We posed to our students four possibilities concerning the relationship between these two disciplines. First, are economics and theology in conflict and is this conflict incommensurable? Thus, one discipline must finally "defeat" the other, or theology must flee to the desert for its viability against encroachments from economics? Second, are they in conflict that is remediable? Thus, we must determine the precise character of the conflict in order to remedy it. Third, can they be cooperative? Might each discipline add something the other needs as mutual and reciprocal partners? Fourth, does theology provide a necessary moral foundation for economics, and economics a practical application of theology? The relationship between them is not so much mutual as it is a relationship of base to superstructure. The answer to all four questions is perhaps, which means that more constantly needs to be said.

We encountered a significant and almost insurmountable barrier right from the beginning. Comparing theology and economics must assume a consistent and coherent subject matter to each discipline. Anyone familiar with either of these fields knows what constitutes the fields themselves is essentially contested, making an exceedingly complex comparison. Economics, ironically, seems more cohesive and unified, centered as it is on the appropriateness of the free market as a defensible institution whose purpose is to allocate scarce resources as efficiently as possible, than does theology centered on its relationship to the church. Modern economists are less in rebellion against the market than modern theologians are against the church. Most neoclassical economists are agreed that "the free market is the most efficient instrument for utilizing resources and effectively responding to needs" (Baumol and Blinder, 1997, 425–526). Nothing unifies theological methodology in the contemporary university in the same way that the market unifies methodology in economics. Most succinctly, economics is "the study of how people and societies deal with scarcity." This is its first principle, and it would not work well without it. It is a social science because it deals with human behavior (Katz and Rosen, 1991, 2). It is based on the premise that individuals respond to incentives and make rational decisions to maximize their satisfaction. Most neoclassical economists would claim that economics is a positive science, "a systematized knowledge concerning what is," as John Neville Keynes put it (Keynes, 1964, 3–4).

Theology, however, presents a more contestable and less easily identifiable subject matter. This is not altogether surprising, for as the theologian John Milbank argues,

> . . . theology has no "proper" subject matter, since God is not an object of our knowledge, and is not immediately accessible. Instead theology must always speak "also" about the creation, and therefore always "also" in the tones of human discourses about being, nature, society, language and so forth. (Milbank, 1997, 3)

Theology's lack of a "proper subject matter" does not finally create an insurmountable barrier in comparing these two fields of study, for theology always uses analogical language to convey truths about God, a language inseparable from that used in economics. Terms such as *redemption, debt, gift, exchange,* and *economy* constitute theological language. Theology and economics do not speak about two separate and autonomous spheres; they cannot be relegated to some rigid late scholastic distinction between the natural and supernatural. However, they both speak about everyday human action—even if they speak about it in radically different, and at times incommensurable, ways. These differing descriptions of human action make possible, and necessitate, a comparison between the two disciplines.

However, the contested identity of theology could not simply be remedied by recognizing that theology itself has no proper subject matter. Theologians differ markedly as to the compatibility not only between theology and economics in general, but Christian theology and capitalism specifically. The latter two fields of study—Christian theology and capitalist economics—constitute the subject of our comparison (and most of our arguments).

We also managed to argue over the important question as to how *value* is produced, and what is meant by value. The second chapter, "The Facts about Values," is our attempt to come to terms with the very different accounts of values, virtues, and the good and goods present in our two disciplines. In these first two chapters, we simply let our agreements and disagreements stand. We do not (because we cannot) resolve the disagreements. Nor do we always show specific economic implications of the different first principles, although we certainly do that indirectly. Our ongoing debates about selling bodily organs and creating a market for adoptable children reflect the different consequences of our first principles. However, the point of these two chapters is not to settle these disputes, but to figure out what they might be, and even if we have sufficient common agreement to have a significant dispute. One implication of our dispute is the possibility that people will find themselves before two different kinds of communities—the market or the church—and seek to determine which one will render their lives intelligible, i.e., whose first principles are compelling.

However, Fox is not sure such a question is warranted. She finds economics not to be wedded to a particular community but to be more of a neutral mechanism for distributing goods under conditions of scarcity. She does not find compelling the assumption that the church and the global market are in any sense competitors.

The first two chapters are an effort to engage in a debate between theology and economics; they are not attempts to offer economic prescriptions or construct a more just global economic order. They are an effort to present, elucidate, and compare "first principles." As Alasdair MacIntyre argues, "Genuinely first principles can have a place only within a universe characterized in terms of a certain determinate, fixed and unalterable ends, ends which provide a standard by reference to which our individual purposes, desires, interests and decisions can be evaluated as well or badly directed. For in the practical life it is the *telos* [end] which provides the *archê*, the first principle of practical reasoning" (MacIntyre, 1995, 7). In other words, practical reasoning requires knowledge of the purpose or end for a discipline or discourse, which will then allow us to recognize its first principle. The first principle is not a free-floating foundation that can make sense without the end. If we do not know the end, which would reflect the best of a particular discourse, we could not know how to begin to reason toward it.

Christian theology has as its end friendship with the Triune God. Its first principle will then entail a natural desire for this vision that includes notions of truth and goodness in ordering our lives toward this end. Practical reasoning about theology and economics then entails showing how our lives move toward this end or away from it within the context of everyday exchanges. This requires a traditioned rational inquiry that draws on the wisdom of those who have come before us. This is part of the virtue of practical wisdom.

Does economics also have an end, and first principle—that generates its universe of discourse? The first two chapters are an effort to discover whether this is the case.

Chapter 3 is my effort to engage in practical reasoning from the perspective of Christian theology's *telos* and *archê*. Because the Eucharist provides the center of the argument for what a theological economy is, readers may very well continue to ask the question Tanner posed. How is this a political engagement with real economic realities and not a flight into some safe sanctuary free from politics? This chapter addresses that question by asking "what makes theology political"? By drawing upon the philosopher Charles Taylor's understanding of practical reason, I hope to show that too much of political theology assumes, following Weber, that politics has more to do with power and its distribution than goodness or truth. The politics assumed throughout this work rests on the belief that truth and goodness are more basic than pure power for our everyday exchanges. I do not see how that could possibly be construed as a counsel of despair. Nor should it be interpreted as a naïve romanticism. Truth and goodness are inescapable because God created this world. But that does not mean we cannot refuse to acknowledge this transcendent reality and act as if all we have is an immanent power to make the world as we see fit, to produce "value." Can anyone actually live that way?

No discussion of the first principles of economics can avoid engaging its chief philosophical architect, Adam Smith. Chapter 4 offers a suggestion as to how theologians could, and should, read him. If Smith does not give us a neutral, universal form of rationality that is independent of contingent political ordering, that is to say, if his work is understood as a form of practical reasoning that assumes an end and first principle, then we can gain insight into his work by viewing him as standing within a traditioned rational moral enquiry, much as we see the church fathers.

The first four chapters discuss the logic of the market; they are an effort to lay out its *archê*. The next four chapters are an attempt to reason practically about the corporation and everyday economic life in terms of Scripture and its tradition of interpretation. For that reason, this work divides into two parts. The first is the logic of the market, an investigation of first principles and ends. The second is corporation and everyday economic life, a traditioned theological inquiry. It examines the significance of first principles and ends for how we think about the corporation, its role in the economy, exchange and interest, and concludes with the economic significance of the central sign of communication in the church: the Holy Eucharist.

Chapter 5, "Corporations and the Ends We Serve," attempts to ask how corporations fit within the divine economy. Some theologians speak of corporations as if they are straight from the pit of hell and once the revolution happens then we will not have them any longer. Others speak of the corporation as if it were a worldly church or a fourth manifestation of the body of Christ. Both types of speech seem to me to be utter nonsense; both neglect the limited role the corporation plays in God's economy by giving it too much capacity for evil or good. This is not to deny that corporations can produce great evil, as we have witnessed first hand with Enron, WorldCom, and Arthur Andersen. Nor is it to deny that they do great good, even moral good, as I try to show with the example of Maytag and other corporations. The difficulty with the corporation occurs when it seeks to be more than it should, when it tries to become a salvific institution. However, this may be more common than we recognize if the only end the corporation serves is "profit maximization." Corporations can be held accountable to this only legal end, but this is not the only end they can serve.

This question will not allow us to leave behind part 1 and the discussion of ends and first principles. It requires us, as theologians, to think about proper ends: what are they? How do natural and supernatural ends relate? When a natural end knows no limits, as profit maximization suggests, then has it not become a "supernatural" entity seeking an infinite end? Interestingly, this is exactly why Aquinas opposed usury. It denied the limited end money could serve by making it serve an end that knew no limits, which was the vice of greed. Is greed good? Is it an inevitable feature of capitalism? Some theologians are too quick to exonerate capitalism from this charge without an adequate account of the vice of greed and the virtues that it trades on—as vices always do—especially charity, justice, and liberality.

Chapter 6 traces the complex history of the usury prohibition, and especially its contemporary interpretation, in order to make the argument that this law can only make sense in terms of these three virtues—charity, justice, and liberality—and their opposition to the vice of greed. The purpose of this chapter is not to argue for a recovery of the usury prohibition per se, but to recover a meaningful discussion on the virtues to which it pointed and the vices against which it worked. Such a focus could have led to a very different result than the recent corporate scandals. In a promiscuous society such as ours, fending off greed and relearning the mortification of the flesh that charity, justice, and liberality require may be the most radical form of politics we could pursue.

Chapter 7 finds the debate among Christian ethicists and theologians as to whether we must be capitalists or (state) socialists misguided and a deterrent from what we should be doing as theologians—which is to ask what difference Christian doctrine and practice make for how we live within the market.

Once again in this chapter, Adam Smith's stoic theology appears; and I pose the question regarding how it relates to Christian theology. I do think that Smith's tradition of economics has as its basis a stoic theology and that this is perpetuated unknowingly by most economists who would deny they were in any sense theological. I try to cite evidence for this in the economists' work. However, even if someone else finds this argument compelling, it does not mean that the church and the market are incompatible. For as Benedict XVI (as Joseph Ratzinger) argued, in the wisdom tradition "the whole of the Torah, Israel's law for living, is now understood as wisdom's self-portrait, as the translation of wisdom into human language and human instruction. A natural consequence of all of this is similarity to Greek thought, to some themes of Platonism, on the one hand, and on the other to the Stoic association of morality with the interpretation of the world as divinely inspired" (Ratzinger, 2003, 151).

Stoicism and Christianity share things in common. I find Smith's stoic theology problematic not because it is stoic, but because of the kind of stoicism it is. It assumes that embodying the virtues is more dangerous to political and economic exchanges than the vices. If this were true, then we would have no adequate end to economic life that would be able to distinguish between pure manipulation and a moral act.

The concluding chapter, "Offering our Gifts," is written with Tripp York. It seeks to address both how Christians might discern what the end to economic exchanges is and what a gift economy would look like. We draw upon the Eucharist as the central form of "exchange" that should render for Christians all other forms of exchange intelligible. This chapter comes from Hauerwas and Wells' excellent volume, *The Blackwell Companion to Christian Ethics*. My hope is that this work will cause the reader to ask the question, "So what? What should I do now?"

Many answers can be given to that question, but one place to begin is to look at that volume and see the forms of faithful common living it represents. In that volume, it is noted that if there is any merit to a "Christian economic vision" that escapes some of the silliness present in church life today, it is in the work being done by the many contributors, and their churches, and communities they represent.

# PART I

## THE LOGIC OF THE MARKET
An Investigation of First Principles

# — 1 —

## PROPHETS AND PROFITS

## Economics and Theology in Conflict?

What are the first principles of economics? To know this we must first ask what is its end. An answer to that question is simple: efficiency. The end of the market is to allocate scarce resources as efficiently as possible. This may seem intrinsically opposed to the end of theology, which is friendship with God, but we should not judge it so too quickly. Efficiency in itself is not a faithless end. Anyone who has worked for an inefficient corporation or institution knows how troubling that can be. The question is how encompassing this end will be. Will it require all other ends to serve it? Are there not reasons for being inefficient in some activities? Can efficiency serve the ultimate end of charity, which characterizes friendship with God and never ends? On the other hand, does the logic of the market entail first principles that exceed the limited purpose of the end of efficiency and subordinate everything to them as necessary means? The following conversation does not answer these questions, but hopes to illumine them.

NANCY FOX: AN ECONOMIST'S DESCRIPTION OF THEOLOGY AND ECONOMICS

### Efficiency, Charity and Justice

Perhaps the first conflict between theology and economics arises as to what constitutes the goal of an economic system. Should efficiency be the goal of an economic system? Neoclassical economists would claim that efficiency is the appropriate goal of an economic system and would even state that such a claim is itself a positive, rather than a normative, statement. This is what economic analysis does; it assesses efficiency, separate from a prescribed normative vision. Theologians are more likely to view justice and charity as the appropriate goal of an economic system. Thus, the U.S. Catholic bishops state,

> Our faith calls us to measure this economy not only by what it produces, but also by how it touches human life and whether it produces or undermines the dignity of the human person. Economic decisions have human consequences and moral content; they help and hurt people, strengthen or weaken family life, advance or diminish the quality of justice in our land. (Stackhouse, 1995, 439)[6]

Examples of these differing perspectives appear regularly in questions of public policy. Should we have a minimum wage? Neoclassical economists say no because it is inefficient and interferes with the allocatable role of the market. Catholic theologians have advocated for more than a minimum wage; they argue for a just wage.

Should health care management be based on the "bottom line?" Neoclassical economists say yes, otherwise no incentive to contain costs exists. Theologians question the appropriateness of placing monetary value on health and life. Moreover, accessibility to health care should be independent of economic status.

Should people be allowed to sell their bodily organs, either while alive or after death? Four thousand people die waiting for organ transplants while another 12,000–15,000 people die each year whose organs could be used. Neoclassical economists find the market a reasonable means of allocating usable organs, which get uselessly buried every year with their "owners." To allow the market to distribute these organs would produce a more efficient system. Everyone has his price; no one is harmed and some are better off. The proposal is Pareto superior.[7] However, some theologians find the marketing of body organs a denial of friendship and charity. Offering organs for a price degrades the human person.

Should corporations strive solely for efficiency? Milton Friedman suggests that the "only social responsibility of business—[is] to use its resources and engage in activities designed to increase its profits." (Friedman, 2006, 9) Of course, even CEO's are suspicious of subordinating all business practices to efficiency. Thus, Bennett Le Bow, CEO of Brooke Group which owns Liggett Group,[8] the smallest of the American tobacco companies recently stated in a commencement address:

> The dual pressures of economics and politics in the business world will frequently challenge your instincts to "do the right things." Resist those pressures. . . . Listen to your moral voices, and do not be afraid to break from the pack, even if it costs you and your company a lot of money.

Although the prioritizing of efficiency makes even business leaders uneasy, economics makes little sense without the assumption that it is the central, if not the sole, purpose of exchange. Theologians subordinate efficiency to questions of charity and justice. Although this is laudable, it often lacks an adequate analysis of the long-term consequences of their vague policy implications on the whole system.

### A View of the Whole System

Theologians and neoclassical economists view individuals differently. Neoclassical economists tend to compartmentalize people, viewing them as economic agents who supply labor and demand goods and services. This allows their disparate practices, desires, needs, and wants to be commodified. In fact, for neoclassical economists, essentially anything can be commodified, which in turn produces a limited vision. For instance, a neoclassical economist's analysis of a worker's wage will ignore its effect on the worker's role as a parent.

Just as neoclassical economists often fail to see the whole person, theologians fail to see the effect of economic change on the whole system. They tend to see only the partial equilibrium, instead of the general equilibrium results. Consider the following two examples (Hirshleifer and Glazer, 1992, 3). First, apartment rates are rising, putting decent housing out of the reach of the poor. A solution centered on justice or charity would advocate freezing the rates. However, the result will be either that landlords skimp on upkeep and repairs creating a dangerous environment, or fewer rental units will be constructed, exacerbating the problem. Second, commercial fishing for tuna kills large numbers of dolphins. A charitable or just response might require fishermen to use special nets that do not harm dolphins. Nevertheless, the response will be that consumers pay more for tuna, and fishermen not bound by U.S. law will take over the tuna trade. The same number of dolphins will still be harmed, and U.S. fishermen and consumers will suffer.

These two problems are real. The proposed solutions are commendable, but because the general equilibrium results are not taken into account, the solutions neither accomplish their intent nor offer helpful policy prescriptions. In fact, they accomplish the opposite of their intent. Such judgments are not often welcome. "Good economic analysis upsets people. It forces people to look at reality from a different perspective than most people use" (Colander, 1991, 5). But this fuller reality needs to be taken into account. While others (including theologians) focus solely on the benefits of a particular policy, neoclassical economists see both the benefits *and the costs.*[9]

*The Language of Value, the Value of Language*

Neoclassical economists and theologians do not speak the same language. They often use the same terms in different ways, resulting in incommensurability. Consider the basic concept of value. Adam Smith made the distinction between value in use, "the utility of some particular object" and value in exchange, "the power of purchasing other goods which possession of that object conveys" (Brue, 1994, 80). He illustrated the importance of this distinction with his famous water-diamond paradox. Water, which is essential to life, has a much higher value in exchange than do diamonds, without which everyone can live. Thus, it is not value-in-use but value-in-exchange that determines a good's value.

Neoclassical economists have more or less accepted Smith's distinctions and have concentrated for two centuries on explaining how value in exchange is determined. The model of supply and demand, successfully set forth by Alfred Marshall in 1890, is invoked to explain the value of everything from cars and apples to body organs and babies.

Theologians eschew this concept of value-in-exchange as determinative, for it lacks any relationship with a good's use. Goods derive their value from their ability to satisfy human needs. It follows that the market does not adequately determine value, which is intrinsic to the good's proper function. The concept of value is intrinsic to the appropriate distribution of income. Christian theologians, drawing upon Acts 4, seem more inclined to Marx's notion that income should be distributed "from each according to his ability to each according to his need." Neoclassical economists, however, change the second part of that aphorism to "to each according to his ability." And this is a version of John Bates Clark's marginal productivity theory of distribution: "distribution of income in society is controlled by a natural law . . . which would give to every agent of production the amount of wealth the agent creates" (Brue, 1994, 281). Insofar as the neoclassical economist insists that income should be distributed according to the value of productivity alone, and theologians to the value involved in satisfying needs, the two disciplines do not share a language of value.

Another example of a difference in language use is the concept of scarcity. As Knight puts it, "the purpose of economic activity is to satisfy wants" (Knight, 1969, 45). The implication of scarcity—insufficient resources to satisfy limitless wants—is that economic decisions always involve choice, which implies opportunity cost. Thus economics can be viewed as "the study of how people make decisions under conditions of scarcity," an analysis of the trade-offs that necessarily result from that scarcity and the implications of the decisions on society.

A third example of incommensurable language use is the contentless criteria by which theologians tend to judge the outcome of any system. Both theologians and neoclassical economists seem to incorporate the notion of "fairness" into outcomes assessment. However, the neoclassical economist will ask if the *process* was fair, while theologians apply fairness to the *outcome* itself. By the neoclassical economist's use of fairness, an outcome is fair (and therefore acceptable) if it is achieved via voluntary actions, mutual consent, and if everyone has a fair chance to get ahead. If these conditions do not hold, then the process is unfair; and the process ought to be remedied. By contrast, a theologian will judge an unfair outcome as that which ought to be remedied. Theologians seek an equality of results, while neoclassical economists seek an equality of opportunity.

### The Roles of Theologians and Economists

Theologians and neoclassical economists have different, but not necessarily contradictory, roles. With respect to economics, the role of the theologian is to "keep the market in its place." Theologians tend to see the market as encroaching upon everything and imposing its logic in some sort of conspiracy. Neoclassical economists find this to be strange, for they view their prescriptions as largely ignored by politicians and the general public. For instance, if theologians are correct, why is it that something as universally agreed upon by neoclassical economists as the harmful effects of a minimum wage are obviously ignored year after year by politicians? The role of the neoclassical economist is not to be unconcerned about justice and charity but to insure that as the problem of economic injustice is addressed, well-informed decisions are made, and the necessary trade-offs in every decision are recognized.

Over twenty years ago, Arthur Okun addressed this important role of the neoclassical economist in analyzing the problem of redistributing income from rich to poor. Okun uses the example of a leaky bucket. Imagine that money is liquid (like water) and that a bucket is used to transport money from rich to poor, but the bucket leaks. As you move the money, some of it is lost. The question is at what point does it become inefficient to use that bucket to move the money. If only one cent is lost for every one dollar moved, everyone would probably find it a worthwhile endeavor. But what if each dollar taken from the rich results in only ten cents redistributed to the poor? Only the most extreme egalitarians would then endorse the process. The difficult case is when twenty to forty cents is lost. Should redistribution take place? Neoclassical economists cannot answer that question; their role is first to point out that the bucket does leak and second to estimate the extent of the leak. Society must make the judgment about what constitutes acceptable leakage, and such judgments should be assisted by theological and moral considerations.

Theologians and neoclassical economists are agreed that the market contains weaknesses. It is not a perfect system. John Paul II has stated,

> There are many human needs which find no place in the market.
> It is a strict duty of justice and truth not to allow fundamental

human needs to remain unsatisfied and not to allow those bur-
dened by such needs to perish. (Stackhouse, 1995, 489)

Would neoclassical economists disagree? Most neoclassical economists recognize John Paul's point. For instance, Baumol and Blinder
state, "The market mechanism is extraordinarily good at promoting
efficiency but not very good at promoting equality" (Baumol and
Blinder, 1997, 425). Or as Blinder more pithily notes in *Hard Heads
and Soft Hearts*, "An unfettered market system shows no mercy. If
there is to be mercy, it must be imposed from the outside" (Blinder,
1987, 21). Even Okun would agree with the theologian's assessment
of the market. "The market needs a place, and the market needs to
be kept in its place." This is a legitimate role for the theologian.

Theology and economics contain significant differences in perspective, use-of-language, and understanding of each discipline's
role, but can we not cooperate and come to a compromise? John
Paul II assists us with this compromise. "The Catholic tradition,"
he states, "calls for a society of work, enterprise, and participation
which is not directed against the market, but demands that the
market be appropriately controlled by the forces of society and by
the state to assure that the basic needs of the whole society are satisfied" (Stackhouse, 1995, 371). Most neoclassical economists would
agree, once we know what constitutes "appropriately controlled."

## STEVE LONG: A THEOLOGIAN'S DESCRIPTION OF THEOLOGY AND ECONOMICS

Nancy Fox has set forth a number of questions and issues that separate theologians and neoclassical economists. I find her analysis of
these differences quite compelling, which makes the task of relating theology and economics more difficult. For if I disagreed with
her assessment, I could simply explain how she has misunderstood
theology, remedy her misunderstanding, and perhaps more easily
find common ground between the two disciplines.

Only one of her descriptions of theology strikes me as errant,
and that is her suggestion that theology tends to be concerned with

vague contentless concepts such as fairness and compassion. She is right to recognize that such concepts are contentless and that a number of theologians tend to invoke them as shibboleths. Nevertheless, the posture some neoclassical economists assume that theirs is a *hard-headed* analysis of the facts that needs to be supplemented by a *soft-hearted* morality or theology simply will not do. Theologians can be as realistic in their analysis of what their discipline requires of others as neoclassical economists can be. Theology is as willing, and in fact more than willing, to produce martyrs for its cause than is economics. And I recognize that my own theological convictions likewise invite others to suffer for them as do those of economists.

### Efficiency, Charity, and Justice

Fox's first significant distinction between economics and theology is the question regarding whether efficiency or charity and justice can, or should, be the goal of economic exchanges. She rightly notes the tension here between a theological economics that subordinates the necessity of exchanges to reflect our participation in God's life and the neoclassical economists' social scientific analysis that merely presents the facts—facts that are claimed to be natural and neutral.

Theologians should not avoid the question of efficiency altogether. No one should argue that the horse-and-buggy industry should have been sustained after the invention of the automobile in order to be charitable to workers in the horse and buggy industry—unless, of course, one lives in Lancaster, Pennsylvania, and/or our obsession with, and utter dependence upon, the automobile results in devastating ecological and social results. Then this well-known example of the economist's apology for more efficient industries over inefficient ones would simply no longer be valid. However, this is a significant point, and one which I think challenges the heart of Fox's defense of economics as merely presenting natural facts. It is not a *natural* fact that the automobile industry is more efficient than horses and buggies or, for that matter, bicycles. Such a claim can be, at most, a contingent historical and social *factum* ("made") based upon what appears most efficient at the moment. And it remains contingent upon the social conditions that make automobiles preferable to other modes of transportation. But precisely because we have a social and historical order that is geared toward the efficiency of the automobile, that industry will indeed appear most efficient. Thus economists constantly mistake what is made at a particular social and historical moment for a natural fact. Insofar as neoclassical economists can recognize the contingent character of all their proposals, their analysis could be helpful. When they deny this, they inevitably become spokespersons for the present distribution of social and political power—whatever it might be—under the illusion that it is natural.

Another question Fox raises is whether all things *should* be assigned a monetary value or not (they obviously *can* be). Neoclassical economists assume that all things have a formal equivalence. Theologians suggest that while human beings do have the ability to give all things monetary value, some things such as virtue, friendship, life with God, family life, etc. should not be valued. To concede such things a value and compare them with others is to distort them. Neoclassical economists are not so dismal that they reject possible incommensurabilities. At a general level we would all agree that family life should not be thought of primarily in terms of its monetary value. But when we move from the general to the particular, economists and theologians soon part company. For instance, should the distribution of health, sex, body organs, and infants be conceded a value that allows them to be efficiently exchanged through a market mechanism? We find neoclassical economists who argue in favor of commodifying all four of these goods.[10] But are not these goods precisely related to family life? If the economic facts suggest that a more efficient method of distributing body organs, sex, health, and unwanted infants is through the market, then are not those theologians (such as myself) who fear the encroachment of the market in all aspects of life justified?

Another issue is the legitimacy of one's "access" to particular goods. Neoclassical economists prescind from questions of whether it is good that certain persons have better access to health care, organ transplants, transportation, etc. simply because of their economic status. Fox obviously has sympathies with a theological perspective grounded in charity and friendship, but she cannot finally embrace this perspective because it lacks a fullness of perspective. She states, "theologians often fail to see the effect of an economic change on the 'whole system.' They tend to see only the partial equilibrium, instead of the general equilibrium results." The result is that the theologian's good intentions create unwarranted and unnecessary suffering whereas the neoclassical economist's efficient intentions produce the unintended consequences of diminishing suffering and increasing usefulness.

I think her characterization of the difference here between theologians and neoclassical economists could very well be correct. To live by a just wage, or to seek to ground economic exchanges in charity and friendship rather than in the negative freedom of modern rights, may very well increase the suffering in the world. The question is so what?—so does living by the principle of not to kill innocent noncombatants or not to commit adultery. Can we not all easily imagine situations where, according to the ethical criteria of the useful, a little direct killing of the innocent, a little discrete adultery might very well increase the pleasure and diminish the pain of mortal existence? But useful for what purpose? The neoclassical economist's analysis can only respond, "for the purpose of increasing pleasure or decreasing pain." And this response demonstrates that economists repeat nineteenth-century moralists who thought that the increase of pleasure and the diminishment of pain could adjudicate moral differences in human action. As a discipline, economics has seldom come to terms with its inextricable connectedness to a particular moral and theological tradition—utilitarianism.

It provides the first principles within which economics works, and to which it always inevitably returns.

### A View of the Whole System

This second issue relates to her third question of "the whole system." Fox argues that theologians fail to see how the whole system works. Once again, I think she adequately characterizes how theology works. Unlike neoclassical economists, theologians do prescind (or should prescind) from setting forth a totalizing schema where the effect of one action can, with clarity and certainty, be traced without remainder to another. This is because our actions, like God's, produce a plenitude that always exceeds our grasp. We do not know the "general equilibrium result." In theology, there is always an eschatological reserve that limits knowledge of the whole. What concerns me about the study of economics is precisely these totalizing claims. Economics claims to see the total whole, which is embodied this time, not in the state (as it was for fascism) but in the natural workings of the market; and then it requires some people to sacrifice for the sake of this totality. Those sacrifices are then justified on the basis of the natural truth of the totality. They are necessary phases toward the best possible outcome assessment, whether they are willed or not. This is doubly ironic in that the basis for this economic analysis is then viewed as individual preference.

### The Language of Value, the Value of Language

Fox's analysis of the different uses of language by theologians and neoclassical economists is particularly illuminating. She suggests that neoclassical economists use terms such as *value* and *scarcity* in a limited and technical sense that laypersons misunderstand. However, does this assume that neoclassical economists have created their own private language that is unavailable to the common person? Or is the appeal to a technical usage a strategy to produce an impenetrable fortress around the scientific study of economics that renders it incapable of interrogation from other disciplines? Scarcity is scarcity. Just because it is grounded in want rather than need does not make the concept difficult to understand. Capitalist economics assumes scarcity, but I shall argue, not as a empirical analysis of the natural. It functions in economics as a metaphysical claim. The economists Baumol and Blinder ask the question, "What is the basic task that economists expect the market to carry out?" Then they answer, "the market resolves THE fundamental problem of the economy: the fact that all decisions are constrained by the scarcity of available resources" (Baumol and Blinder, 1997, 49). Notice the language invoked, "all decisions are constrained by scarcity." While this assumes a scarcity of resources, it also assumes a more fundamental scarcity in an individual consumer to consume the infinite commodities which could possibly satisfy her or his infinite desires. It is related to that other metaphysical foundation for modern economics, Wieser's discovery (should we say invention) of opportunity costs. The moment I choose "x" I forego the possibility of all non-x's and they become to me a "cost" never to be recovered. I must first want everything in order for it to then be a "cost" to me.

This account of human agency is thoroughly modernist and metaphysical in that it fits well the bifurcated subject found in Kantian ethics. The agent exists in a noumenal realm defined by freedom and the infinite. The agent also exists in a phenomenal realm grounded in desire and finite sensibility. The possibility of the agent's action is grounded in the infinite, particularly through freedom. The moment the agent actually acts, however, that freedom is constrained by finitude and sensibility. All action then is viewed as a loss, a negation of an original infinite potential. All action assumes death. This metaphysical foundation for economics is consistent with what Christian theology has traditionally called sin, especially the vice of *pleonexia* (greed) where we have an infinite desire for finite goods. If scarcity is "THE economic problem" that generates economic analysis, then does it not depend upon the proliferation and perpetuation of the Christian vice of *pleonexia* for its viability? To that extent, economic analysis works against any understanding of holiness where we are to learn and cultivate a finite desire for finite goods and an infinite desire for the only infinite good—God. Modern economics does not merely assume sinfulness, it needs it. It would not work without the proliferation of disordered desire.

### The Roles of Theologians and Economists

In truth, Professor Fox does not sense the need to subordinate theology to economics, as I seek to subordinate economics to theology. The relationship she poses between theology and economics is much more modest than mine. She is more than willing to concede that economics cannot answer every question about what society should do. When it comes to the "should," she is more than willing to allow the theologians to contribute to society's shared goals. And she is willing to serve those goals as long as we recognize the costs they incur and do not remain sentimental about charity and justice without pain and suffering. She simply seeks an autonomous space for neoclassical economists—as social scientists—to ply their trade and achieve their limited objectives, to present the facts of the costs and benefits in economic exchanges. Why then am I, as a theologian, unwilling to concede her this simple space?

The reason I continue to insist that the theologian's task is to keep the market in its place is precisely because, as she noted, I do think the market has become a counter-church in modern and post-modern society. It has become the one institution which people look to for salvation. The very name, "the global market," causes a theological pause. Of course, though, Christian theology suggests only one institution is truly *kat' ôlos*, ("according to the whole," Catholic or global), and that institution is the church. At the same time that the church seems to be dissolving into national identities, another social institution has taken its place to offer a global vision to persons across national boundaries and ethnic particularities.

Because I do confess that "I believe in the one, holy, Catholic, and apostolic church," I cannot concede any autonomous space for a putatively neutral and natural analysis of what I find to be a competing catholic institution—the global market. That cannot help but make Professor Fox nervous, and I recognize it. Surely she wonders whether my reliance on a Catholic ecclesiology is not just as totalizing as I have implicitly accused neoclassical economists of being in their capacity of serving the global market. Curiously, we share a nervousness about the totalizing impulse in the social institutions we each serve.[11]

### Nancy Fox: Conclusion

Both theologians and neoclassical economists appear to agree that the market is the best way for an economic system to achieve efficiency. In *Centesimus Annus*, John Paul II wrote, " . . . the free market is the most efficient system for utilizing resources and effectively responding to need." His words are remarkably similar to Baumol and Blinder's analysis of the market system. Despite this area of agreement, there remain many spheres of conflict, which are exacerbated by differences in language and goals. At times we appear to have portrayed the relationship between Catholic theology and market economics as a zero sum game (what Long calls "incommensurability") where there is room for only one winner. Certainly, Long hints at that when he writes that "the market has become a counter-church in modern and post-modern society." Long alleges that a market economy imposes itself upon all facets of life. Yet, he never explained just how the market was able to impose itself and achieve this successful hegemony. This alleged imposition neglects the fact that neoclassical economists do recognize not only the limits of the market but also its failings.

Possibly the most significant source of conflict is the sheer ignorance of one discipline of the other. If this is true, we are indeed fortunate, because that ignorance can be remedied. As an example, consider the neoclassical economists' fixation with efficiency, a concept that certainly appears to be cold-hearted. How could anyone oppose the minimum wage or price supports for necessities? Few outside the profession (and probably some within) understand that:

> Efficiency is important not because it is a desirable end in itself, but because it enables us to achieve all other goals to the fullest possible extent. Whenever a market is out of equilibrium, there is waste, and waste is always a bad thing. Whenever there is waste, there must exist ways to improve on our current situation. (Frank, 1998, 77)

Even if the church and the market can agree with this analysis of the importance of efficiency, they may disagree, not only about what "other goals" we should strive for, but also whether or not they are achievable at all.

As commendable as the goals of friendship, charity, and fairness are, it is naive to expect people to behave in a way that they will be realized. The description of a neoclassical economist as one who knows the price of everything and the value of nothing is unwarranted. Neoclassical economists recognize that people respond to incentives, and the promise of rewards in the world to come is insufficient to inspire selfless behavior. (Consider the present value of such rewards!) We should not be content with a system that allows some to dine on caviar while others starve. But theology offers no system that would address these problems successfully, let alone one that would not also create new difficulties.[12]

Nevertheless, Long and I identified issues on which we are in agreement, although occasionally that agreement was somewhat reluctant. (1) Market exchange is necessary. (2) Economics and theology are related at some level, although we disagree as to the exact level and degree of commensurability. (3) Friendship is as important as efficiency. (4) There are aspects of our lives on which the market should have no bearing—some things should not be "commodified."

(5) The government that governs least governs best, as the classical economists would put it. (6) We can find God in all things.

There continue to be matters on which we will never reach a consensus. (1) Some things are facts and they occur naturally (such as insatiable greed.) Long contends that many economic "facts" are instead values that arise out of a historical and moral context. (2) Long would exclude many more goods and services from the market than I would. He would never allow a market for body organs, for example, even if lives were saved at no one's expense. (3) I would allow for the validity of the individual's making his own "rational" decisions under more circumstances than would Long.

A final word on goals. What are the "other goals" that efficiency allows us to attain—specifically, can economics assume the goal of Thomas Aquinas, which is a vision of God as a true end? The answer to this last question must be no. The concept of a universe "with a mysterious aspect that cannot be completely comprehended," (a description one of our students, Michael Arnold, wrote of theology), is alien to economics. In this sense, neoclassical economists are guilty of the sin of hubris, as they believe they can describe and analyze the "general equilibrium" effects of anything on the economic system. This schism between the "Great Economy," the one beyond human comprehension, and the "little economy" in which we live daily, is insurmountable.

# — 2 —

## THE FACTS ABOUT VALUES

If efficiency is the true end of economics and friendship with God that of Christian theology, then are their first principles "the individual will to create value" and the "journey to discover virtue" respectively? That is to say, economists assume that the basic form of action is an individual who chooses, and in so choosing produces value. Whereas theologians assume that value cannot be produced for the good can only be discovered; it is discovered by seeking God above all things. The basic form of human action then is not the acting will, but the reception of gift within the context of a journey. That very journey will require the cultivation and reception of virtues. The cultivation of virtue is what theologians call "natural" or "moral" virtue. The reception of virtue is what they call "infused" or "supernatural" virtue. The latter comes as a gift and not as an accomplishment. The former can be acquired but, when the latter is received, even the nature of the moral virtues is reordered to its true end. For Christian theology, this gift is received through the church, particularly through the Word and Sacraments that allow us to participate in the life of Christ. Values or virtues? This is one of the important questions a conversation between economists and theologians must address.

A headline in *The New York Times* read "Market Puts Price Tags on the Priceless" (Mansnerus, 1998, 1). The article discussed the supply of, and demand for, children in the marketplace of adoption. Such an article raises the question—does everything have a price, or are some things *priceless*? Economists are often accused of knowing the price of everything and the value of nothing. They can tell us what the costs are for our policies, but they cannot tell us why some policies might be better than others—despite the costs incurred. Theologians, however, are often accused of proclaiming the value of everything while overlooking the price incurred for living out those values. They denounce the market's propensity toward putting a price tag on everything without recognizing that moral and theological positions will always require someone to pay. But bringing theologians and economists into a conversation about value is an arduous task.

Although they both invoke this term, it is unclear that they define and use it with sufficient commonality so that they can fruitfully converse with each other. In fact, some theologians have argued that the moral life cannot be spoken of in terms of values at all. As Stanley Hauerwas has put it, "Used cars have value, people shouldn't." Rather than value, these theologians seek to recover the language of virtue, a language that was rendered obsolete as sociologists and religious ethicists turned to the language of value. In this chapter, we investigate the different ways in which economists and theologians define and use the term *value*.

Section 1 is a brief overview of the evolution of the economist's concept of value. Section 2 discusses the language of value from a theological perspective. Section 3 presents a critique of the economist's concept of value. Section 4 presents an alternative to the language of value in the language of virtue. Section 5 examines the propriety of market exchange; and section 6 suggests that such propriety does not yet answer the underlying theological questions.

SECTION 1

THE EVOLUTION OF THE ECONOMIST'S CONCEPT OF VALUE

NANCY FOX

Any misunderstanding about the economist's definition of value should be easily cleared up by a study of Adam Smith, who made the distinction between "value in use" and "value in exchange" over two hundred years ago. He defined value in use as "the utility of some particular object" and value in exchange as "the power of purchasing other goods which possession of that object conveys" (Brue, 1994, 80). Economists since that time have, more or less, accepted Smith's distinction and have concentrated—for the two centuries since—on explaining how value in exchange is determined. The model of supply and demand, which Alfred Marshall developed in 1890, is invoked to explain the value of everything from cars to apples to body organs to babies. Economists have focused for so long on a theory of value of exchange (as opposed to use), that they have essentially eliminated the distinction between the two, dropping the qualifying "in exchange" from the jargon. The theory of value in exchange became the theory of value; eventually, value became "price," and the theory of value became the theory of price. If one is not familiar with this evolution, it is easy to conclude that economists view the value of everything in terms of its price, i.e. money. This is an unfortunate interpretation because it is inaccurate. Economists do not eschew the concept of value in use, rather they choose not to investigate its foundations.

Once economists accepted Smith's distinction, they focused on explaining the determinants of value in exchange and left it to philosophers and theologians to debate value in use. However, for over one hundred years they were perplexed by what became known as the "diamond water paradox." Although Smith distinguished between value in use and value in exchange, he was unable to explain how they were related. "The things which have the greatest value in use," (he suggests water as an example), "have frequently little or no value in exchange; those which have the greatest value in exchange," (here he offers diamonds as an example), "have frequently little or no use value" (Brue, 1994, 80).

Like other early classical economists, Smith offered a theory of value based on cost of production—independent of demand. The relative value of a good depends on the labor necessary to produce it. If a shirt requires two person-hours and a cart requires twenty person-hours, then a cart has ten times the value in exchange as a shirt. For Smith, demand did not have any influence on the value of goods. If we use the "pearl" analogy, the question arises: do pearls have value because people need to dive for them, or do people dive for pearls because they have value? For the classical economists, pearls have value because people have to dive for them.

David Ricardo extended and broadened Smith's theory. He recognized that a good must have use value in order to have value in exchange. This utility, a subjective want satisfying power, does not measure exchange value but is necessary for it. Whereas the classical economists believed that value was derived from cost of production, exclusive of utility—the later economists, the marginalists, believed exactly the opposite. William Stanley Jevons wrote, "value depends entirely in utility" (Jevons, 1888, 1–2; Brue, 1994, 250). For the marginalists, people dive for pearls because they derive utility from them.

The marginalists developed the law of diminishing marginal utility: the more of a good a consumer has, the less utility he derives from an additional unit—which solved Smith's diamond water paradox. Although the total utility of water is greater than the total utility of diamonds, the marginal utility of diamonds is greater than the marginal utility of water. Thus, a rational consumer will prefer all water to all diamonds but would prefer an additional diamond to an additional unit of water. Value in exchange derives from the

value of the marginal unit. Carl Menger emphasized the irrelevance
of cost of production to the determination value, ". . . whether a
diamond was found accidentally or was obtained from a diamond
pit with the employment of a thousand days of labor is completely
irrelevant for its value" (Menger, 1950, 146–47; Brue, 1994, 260).

In *Principles of Economics* (1890), Alfred Marshall synthesized the
two apparently conflicting views of the determinants of value into a
coherent and lasting model of supply and demand. Supply, which is
derived from the cost of production, and demand, which is derived
from utility, together determine price—the value in exchange. To
assert that one or the other is the sole determinant of value is akin
to "disputing whether it is the upper or the under blade of a pair of
scissors that cuts a piece of paper" (Marshall, 1920, 348). The "Mar-
shallian scissors" has remained the prevailing model of the determinant of price for over a hundred years.

SECTION 2

FROM VIRTUES TO VALUES

STEVE LONG

Although Adam Smith produced the decisive definition of value
that would be incorporated into the discipline of economics, the
term itself has a more ancient lineage. It shows up in English manu-
scripts as early as the fourteenth century to designate an "amount
of some commodity, medium of exchange, etc. which is considered
to be equivalent for something else" (*OED*). Value first seems to be
used to define economic exchange. But the term *value* was also used
in the sixteenth century to designate a martial form of life. A man
of value was a man of valor. His worth or value was related to his
efficacy in combat. Here value is related to military virtue. Value
was also related to an estimation of things in terms of their goodness, where this estimate was assumed to belong to God alone. So,
in 1380 the English theologian and reformer, John Wycliffe used the
term by stating that "God keepeth things after their value, for if

anything be better, God maketh it to be better." This conception of value can be contrasted with that of Thomas Hobbes who, in 1651, conflated the commodity, military, and moral conceptions of value when he wrote,

> The value, or WORTH of a man, is as of all other things, his price; that is to say, so much as would be given for the use of his power: and therefore is not absolute; but a thing dependant on the need and judgment of another. . . . And as in other things, so in men, not the seller, but the buyer determines the price. For let a man, as most men do, rate themselves at the highest value they can; yet their true value is no more than it is esteemed by others. (Hobbes, 1983, 115)

Here the term value no longer assumes a theological context but merely an anthropological one. God does not give things their value—including the worth of a human being. That estimation belongs to humanity, and it varies. Of course, this is momentous because Hobbes is the first political thinker to give us the contrast between civil society and nature. Civil society arises out of nature precisely by its ability to give value to things rather than merely take value as given. Here are the intellectual origins for the development of modern society.

We already see present in this assumption the distinction Smith will make famous between value in exchange: a value based on what is esteemed by others, and a value in use, a value that still assumes that certain objects are good because they are esteemed not by us, but by God. That is to say, they have an intrinsic value based upon their function within a theological framework. The latter slowly disappears in the modern world until we find its logical conclusion in the work of an economist like Alfred Marshall, who proclaimed in 1890, "The desire to put mankind in the saddle is the mainspring of most economic study" (Skidelsky, 1994, 170). Humanity is now in the saddle determining its own direction. Thus we need not rely on any false notions of the intrinsic worth of things. We ourselves determine that. The assumption that humans will gives things their value is ultimately associated with the death of God, or should we more accurately say—the need to murder "God" for the sake of our own freedom to will.

Friedrich Nietzsche seems to be the first philosopher to recognize the momentous transformation that occurred once the modern era allowed politics and economics to be based fundamentally on the power of the human will to give the world its value. In *The Gay Science*, Nietzsche sends a "madman" into the marketplace crying out, "I seek God, I seek God." Surely the fact that Nietzsche sets the context for a search for the missing God in the marketplace is no accident. It is precisely the logic of the marketplace that has contributed to the missing reality once called God. In fact, this God is not only missing, this God is dead because God has been murdered. And what the madman finds disconcerting is that those in the marketplace do not yet recognize the greatness of their deed in having destroyed this God. They simply yell and laugh at the madman, until the madman reveals to the persons in the marketplace where the missing God is.

> "Whither is God" he cried. "I shall tell you. We have killed him—you and I. All of us are his murderers. But how have we done this? How were we able to drink up the sea? Who gave us the sponge to wipe away the entire horizon? What did we do when we unchained this earth from its sun? Whither is it moving now? Whither are we moving now? Away from all suns? Are we not plunging continually? Backward, sideward, forward, in all directions? Is there any up or down left? Are we not straying as through an infinite nothing? Do we not feel the breath of empty space? Has it not become colder? Is not night and more night coming on all the while? . . . God is dead. God remains dead. And we have killed him. . . . What was holiest and most powerful of all that the world has yet owned has bled to death under our knives." (Kaufman, 1983, 97)

Nietzsche recognized that a titanic will to power had rendered God so utterly useless that a last and final crucifixion had occurred. All that remains for us to do is to create new gods who might be able to help us control this incredible power for charitable purposes.

Because I think Nietzsche is correct in revealing to us that the power let loose in the modern world becomes disconnected from any account of truth or goodness, I have to push Professor Fox's argument a bit more than she is willing to do. The reason economists fail to explore the concept of "value in use" is because they choose not to—relegating it to the preserve of theologians and moralists. Instead, the domination of exchange values over use values is a sign of the rise of a will to power that creates a society where God not only becomes unnecessary, God must be policed out of public and political life. Must economists not only prescind from explorations of use value, but also actually deny such values exist in order to produce a science based on exchange value alone? I have to raise the following question: does the acceptance of Marshall's model imply a human power to give values to things, a power that implies the death of god?

SECTION 3

AN ECONOMIST'S CRITIQUE OF THE ECONOMIST'S CONCEPT OF VALUE

NANCY FOX

Economists have accepted Marshall's model, so today they do not engage much in critiques of the theory of value. Critics of economics tend to analyze the validity of value theory; curiously, they have an accurate grasp of the economic theory. Those aspects of the market that are perceived by critics as negatives are the very characteristics of the market that economists believe are its strengths. So we will present the economist's concept of value as perceived by noneconomists and then proceed to analyze the differences.

How does the market function to define value?

... the value of a commodity is defined as its exchange value, often referred to as its market value, when it is traded in a laissez-faire market. ... From the individual point of view, the value of a commodity is defined as either the sum of money the holder will accept in order to relinquish it, or the sum of money the potential holder will pay in order to acquire it. (Radin, 1996, 3)

Radin captures the economist's concept of value accurately with just one mistake. Value in exchange is neither the sum which the holder will accept nor the sum the potential consumer is willing to pay. If  these two sums are not equal there will be no exchange, because the value to the seller is different from the value to the consumer. Value in exchange is defined to be the price at which quantity supplied equals quantity demanded, the equilibrium price, where the sum the holder will accept equals the sum the potential consumer is willing to pay. "The simple formula, 'The people want it, and the law of supply and demand does the rest,' explains everything." To explore further "why the people want it, or just who the people are that want it, or why they can make their wants effective" (Cooley, 1913, 547) will not add significantly to a measurement of the value of exchange. It might, however, support or contradict the validity of the result or the implication of the result for public policy.

In deriving demand functions, economists generally take a consumer's preferences as given. There is little discussion of the origin of these preferences; it is assumed that "these wants spring from the inscrutable depths of the private mind ... it has not been customary to recognize that they are the expression of an institutional development" (Cooley, 1913. 546). Cooley may be forgiven this observation, as he wrote in 1913, but others have echoed this criticism. Certainly, when economists focus on the determinants of equilibrium price, they do not delve into the determinants of consumer preferences. But to allege that economists as a profession have ignored the determinants of consumer preferences is to ignore the work of Veblen, Leibenstein, and Galbraith, to name three.

Harvey Liebenstein did extensive work that identified societal determinants of consumer preferences, where a person's demand depends in part on other consumers' demand, namely the bandwagon effect and the snob effect. In the bandwagon effect, consumers demand a good because they want to be part of the crowd or to indulge in a fad. Fashion is an obvious example of the bandwagon effect at work; demand increases as more individuals consume the good. The snob effect, where consumers demand a good because it is exclusive, is the opposite. In this case, quantity demanded is higher when fewer people own the good. Membership in an exclusive club is an example.

Although Liebenstein analyzed the theoretical effects of these forces on demand, Veblen had, in fact, identified them decades earlier. Veblen coined the phrases "conspicuous consumption" and "conspicuous leisure" to describe the phenomena of people making consumption and leisure decisions to impress others. "Since the consumption of these more excellent goods [the best food, drink, clothes, furniture, for example] is an evidence of wealth, it [consumption of these goods] becomes honorific. . . . Conspicuous consumption of valuable goods is a means of reputability. . . . The only practicable means of impressing one's pecuniary ability on these unsympathetic observers of one's everyday life is an unremitting demonstration of ability to pay" (Veblen, 1934, 74–75, 87) .

Galbraith questioned the legitimacy of the assumption that wants originate with the consumer; he believes instead that "as a society becomes increasingly affluent, wants are increasingly created by the process by which they are satisfied" (Galbraith, 1976, 126). Both the desire to consume to acquire or maintain prestige plus modern advertising contribute to productions creating the wants it seeks to satisfy. "Consumer wants can have bizarre, frivolous, or even immoral origins, and an admirable case can still be made for a society that seeks to satisfy them. But the case cannot stand if it is the process of satisfying wants that creates want" (Galbraith, 1976, 122). The claim that marketing does much to shape consumer preferences echoes Knight's observation of forty years earlier. "The wants which an economic system operates to gratify are largely produced by the workings of the system itself" (Galbraith, 1976, 46).

Allegations that economists have ignored the sources of consumer preferences are unfounded. The origin of consumer preferences, however, is irrelevant to the economist's concept of value in exchange, which is derived from consumer preferences *regardless of its source.* The legitimacy or desirability of the market outcome, however, may depend on the sources of those preferences.

Two other characteristics of preferences should be noted. First, economists consider consumers' wants, not their needs. As Knight puts it, "the economic problem [is] how to employ the existing and available supplies of all sorts of resources, human and material, natural and artificial, in producing the maximum *amount of want-satisfaction*" (Knight, 1969, 34). Economists' reliance on wants instead of needs comes in part because they are unable to define and measure needs. Knight explains that "what is really necessary, the physiological requisites for the maintenance of life . . . turns out on examination to be hopelessly ambiguous." He suggests the alternative standard of "what is 'socially necessary,' or a 'decent minimum.'" But even that standard "seems to be closed to any objectively grounded differentiation between the making of a living and any other kind or portion of human activity" (Knight, 1969, 24–25).

Elizabeth Anderson views the consideration of wants instead of needs as a serious shortcoming in economic analysis:

> [The] . . . market . . . is a want regarding institution. What it responds to is "effective demand," that is, desires backed up by money or the willingness to pay for things. Commodities are exchanged without regard for the reasons people have in wanting them. This fact has two implications. First, it means that the market does not respond to needs as such and does not draw any distinction between urgent needs and intense desires. Second, the

market does not draw any distinction between reflective desires, which can be backed up by reasons or principles, and mere matters of taste. Since it provides no means for discriminating among the reasons people have for wanting or providing things, it cannot function as a forum for the expression of principles about the things traded on it. . . . The market provides individual freedom from the value judgments of others. It does not regard any one individual's preferences as less worthy of satisfaction than anyone else's, as long as one can pay for one's satisfaction. But it provides this freedom at the cost of reducing people's preferences, from the market's point of view, to mere matters of taste, about which it is pointless to dispute. (Anderson, 1993, 182)

Second, all consumers' preferences do not count equally in the market. Consumers with sufficient income to act on their preferences are the ones who determine demand. Marshall recognized the importance of income as a determinant of individual demand, and hence of market demand, in 1876 (Marshall, 1876, 128). This construct effectively eliminates those without income from the market, both as consumers, once the market has been established, and also in determining the market itself. Insofar as it is desirable for all consumers to count, this is a shortcoming in determining exchange value.

Those who believe that economists are concerned only with the exchange value of a good are accurate in this observation. Marshall noted that "the machinery of exchange is not concerned with any other of their [goods and services] properties" (Marshall, 1876, 125). However, not to be concerned with something is different from denying its existence. For example, to consider labor a "commodity" that is exchanged in the market for a price is not to demean personhood. It is to compartmentalize people and to focus on a particular dimension of their lives without necessarily devaluing the other dimensions. The complexity of human behavior and society does not eliminate the need for this type of economic analysis; it makes it more important, as Marshall says, "... the complexity and intricacy of social phenomena afford no reason for dispensing with the aid of the economic organon in its proper place; on the contrary they increase the necessity for it" (Marshall, 1885, 163). Marshall goes even a step farther, by claiming that sound economic analysis makes it easier to deal with the other dimensions of the problem:

> ... by introducing systematic and organized methods of reasoning, it [economics] enables us to deal with this one side of the problem [motives, actions that have a money price] with greater force and certainty than almost any other side.... Having done its work, it retires and leaves to common sense the responsibility of the ultimate decision; not standing in the way of, nor pushing out any other kind of knowledge, not hampering common sense ... helping where it could help, and of the rest keeping silent. (Marshall, 1885, 164)

### Section 4
### From Values to Virtues
### Steve Long

The silence of the economist on the question of the ultimate source for value may not be as productive as Marshall suggested. Economists might be reduced to silence on this question precisely because "the rest" of the picture—the role of politics, theology, and morality—has been scripted into a metanarrative that neoclassical economics provides for contemporary culture. That is to say, the understanding of value the economist puts forth too easily becomes the standard to which political, moral, and religious value is reduced. This, of course, is not always the economist's fault; it is the inability of theologians, moralists, and politicians to resist this dominant paradigm that renders their values subordinate to the overarching architectonic of the economist's values.

Once objects in the world are assumed to receive their value only through the estimation given them by the human will, then this understanding of value becomes definitive not only for an autonomous social science of human action such as economics, but also for theology and morality as well. This is clearly seen in the work of Friedrich Hayek. Hayek argued that no common telos (or end) for a religious and/or moral life is permissible if we are to have the liberty that capitalism insures. As it is in the market, so it should be in both the religious and the moral realm. We must respect the individual and see to "the recognition of his own views and tastes as supreme in his own sphere" (Hayek, 1994, 17). In truth, we no longer have a common telos that gives human creatures direction. Instead we all go the way of our own choosing. Everything remains open only to be given value by each individual's will.

Understanding the moral and religious life, under the designation of value, conflicts with an earlier understanding of the moral and religious life under the designation of virtue. Virtue designated an excellence that assumed a common telos rooted in a presumption of what constitutes a good, true, and beautiful social and political life. In other words, the moral life was not a function of individuals making decisions based on utility preferences. Instead, the moral life required a common conception of a good life and the virtues were those actualized dispositions, cultivated habits, and embodied practices that allowed someone to achieve the excellences of that particular form of the good life. The moral life had a direction.

What counts as a virtue depends then primarily on the underlying conception of a good and true life. If the example of a good life is Odysseus, certain excellences will prevail that will give morality a shape that differs if the example of the good life is Jesus. But the moral life cannot be set forth without this common conception of what constitutes the good, and such an account of the good is never a matter of that titanic power which is unencumbered human choice. It is instead, the result of a gift or inheritance. Tradition passes down to us the vision of the good that makes possible the cultivation of virtues—those excellences that allow us to appropriate that good. This account of tradition is not passive but is more akin to being moved by music. The beauty of music causes our bodies to respond; we tap our feet, nod our heads, move our bodies in ways consistent with the music we hear. It is the music that makes us move, but it is also our own agency that acts; we are the ones who tap, nod, and shake. Tradition bears a similar eros. It is an inherited pattern which, at the same time, becomes ours once we move our bodies in ways that allow us to embody for ourselves these patterns which are more than ourselves.

In a community striving for excellence based on a common conception of the good, economics must be a means toward that end and never an end in itself. Daily exchanges are necessary as a condition of human existence. Without such exchanges, life ends. Thus, the theological and moral question is not if we should enter into exchanges, but how we do so. Can we enter into the necessary exchanges for daily sustenance in such a way that these means do not conflict with the ends we seek to serve? Any answer to that question requires the particular end to be set forth.

For instance, if the end of human creation is as Thomas Aquinas suggested—friendship with God—and if friendship with God entails the virtue of charity toward God and neighbor, then this common end raises questions about certain economic means of distribution such as are found in arguments about the "marketplace of adoption" or "the market for bodily organs." These arguments propose that a more efficient form of finding parents to adopt children, or organs for those waiting for them, can occur if the price mechanism became the instrument that facilitated the exchanges. Relying on charitable organizations and state regulations entails an inefficient system. But "efficiency" and "inefficiency" function in a purely formal way here that assumes the economist's value and reads into it what is obviously an inescapable political, moral, and religious matter. That is to say, parents as consumers of marketable commodities, that is, children, are to be given those commodities based on price and willingness/ability to pay. The value of the family becomes the value of the price mechanism. Even if this mechanism facilitates more efficient exchanges, that is, even if it matches more potential consumers with available commodities, something seems to have been lost in the way we now speak of adoption and family.

What is lost? The virtues involved in being a family. Family is one institution free from marginalist rationality. We do not (yet) make decisions about our children and parents based on questions of marginal returns. I do not invest in my children's education or health care because of any potential financial return on my investment. I make such sacrifices for love's sake because it is good to do so. To lose the ability to recognize this relationship between charity and goodness is to lose the notion of the family. Even if it is inefficient, such a loss would make us all less human.

If the moral and religious life is understood as the cultivation and reception of virtues embedded in traditions, then the assumption that morality is about values must be rejected. Rejecting such an assumption is no easy task; for the argument that theology is about values has itself become a tradition that beckons us to respond. To respond to this tradition, however, requires a self-deception. It requires that we respond to a tradition that denies itself as a tradition under the false assumption that the moral life is nothing more than the values we choose for ourselves based on the congruity of our own interest with our own reasons.

The great patriarch of such an understanding of rationality was Max Weber, the father of modern social science. Weber gave us one of the first sciences of human action that refused to correlate human action with any substantive account of a good life. Instead, he used the term *rational* to designate that human action where one's ideas and one's interests were congruent. This rational type of human action was developed in opposition to value, affectual, or traditional forms of action. Value forms of action were of such a type that the action was pursued under some law or principle. Affectual assumed a form of human action where the passions alone moved the person. Traditional forms were those that sought to reproduce earlier forms of life to preserve them in the present and pass them on into the future (Weber, 1978, 24–26). Although all these forms of action were types on a continuum, the "rational" form of action was understood as that where one's ideas and interests congrued, a congruence that Weber does not find in value, affectual, or traditional forms of action. Thus, Weber's account of rational human action fits well with the anthropology underlying the marginalist revolution. A rational action is one where individuals make choices based on "the extra satisfaction gained by a consumer from a small increment in the consumption of a commodity." Religious and moral action based on something other than exchange value becomes, for Weber, the irrational remainder.

Through the work of Ernst Troeltsch, Weber's conception of rational action became the dominant form of Christian Ethics in both Europe and North America. His influential *Social Teaching of the Christian Churches* addressed the social question in terms of Weberian rationality. The question that Troeltsch raises in this work is how the formal spirit of the Christian churches can congrue with the actual, material reality that constitutes the social. In other words, can the Christian idea be congruent with social interests? To answer this question he creates a typology, like Weber, of three different types—the church, the sect, and the mystic. Although Troeltsch's own theology is clearly congruent with the latter, he nevertheless argues that only the first type can truly give us a social and political teaching. Only where the original religious idea is compromised with material and social interests can a social teaching result. Troeltsch's work then gives rise to a dominant tradition of Christian ethics in the United States carried on by Reinhold and H. Richard Niebuhr that also measures the effectiveness of an ethics by correlating the religious idea with societal interests; all other forms of Christian ethics are then compared against this standard of rationality and often found wanting and thus dismissed as "sectarian."

Niebuhr repeats Weber's subordination of ethics and politics to this marginalist rationalization of human action. Weber recognized that if ideas were to be correlated to material interests then those ideas had to bear the marks of "responsibility" to those interests rather than carry on with an irresponsible "ethic of ultimate ends" that advocated the good without compromising it with the useful. As Weber put it,

> No ethics in the world can dodge the fact that in numerous instances the attainment of "good" ends is bound to the fact that one must be willing to pay the price of using morally dubious means or at least dangerous ones—and facing the possibility or even the probability of evil ramifications. From no ethics in the world can it be concluded when and to what extent the ethically good purpose "justifies" the ethically dangerous means and ramifications. The decisive means for politics is violence. (Weber, 1958, 121).

In other words, the good cannot be achieved through virtue. Virtuous means do not result in a good end. To achieve whatever good we can, we must subordinate the good to the useful; that is, to those means that may not be good themselves but are the best we can do given the tragic scarcity that defines our lives.

This complex metaphysical understanding of human action bears the particularity of a philosophical position known as stoicism. It assumes that "human finitude is an impassible barrier to the actualizing of the good life in the human world" (Milbank, 1997, 235). Instead, there are ideals or essences which one must conform to even though those ideals will not necessarily actualize the good in history. Conformation to those ideals results in unintended consequences. But the all-ruling Providence uses these unintended consequences for a universal plan. It was this stoic philosophy which was the heart of Adam Smith's, *The Theory of Moral Sentiments*. Smith stated,

> The ancient stoics were of the opinion, that as the world was governed by the all-ruling providence of a wise, powerful and good

God, every single event ought to be regarded, as making a necessary part of the plan of the universe, and as tending to promote
the general order and happiness of the whole: that the vices and
follies of mankind, therefore, made as necessary a part of this
plan as their wisdom or their virtue; and by that eternal art which
educes good from ill, were made to tend equally to the prosperity
and perfection of the great system of nature. (Smith, 1982, 36)

Smith goes on to argue that this does not lessen our distaste for
disagreeable passions, but instead through this the all-ruling Providence teaches us sympathy; we recognize and are repelled from
vice even though we see that it cannot harm Providence's plan.

Smith's stoicism in *The Theory of Moral Sentiments* is the basis for
his "doctrine of unintended consequences" in *The Wealth of Nations*.
There he argued,

By preferring the support of domestic to that of foreign industry,
[a merchant] intends only his own security; and by directing that
industry in such a manner as it produce may be of the greatest
value, he intends only his own gain, and he is in this, as in many
other cases, led by an invisible hand to promote an end which was
no part of his intention. Nor is it always the worse for the society that it was no part of it. By pursuing his own interest he frequently promotes that of the society more effectually than when
he really intends to promote it. (Smith, 1965, 423)

Interests, values, and virtues run together in Smith's world, and all
can do so precisely because of an underlying theology of providence.
His market mechanism does produce a kind of virtue—stoic virtue.
If someone is convinced that stoicism is the morally and theologically best form of life, the theology that undergirds capitalist economics should be received congenially. If, however, other forms of
the good life compel one, then the neoclassical economist's conception of value must be refused. It cannot be allowed a superior

position over other kinds of virtues, even though it is the dominant form in our culture.

I think that the economist's concept of value reveals that this account of theological rationality and this stoic doctrine of unintended consequences have now nearly become our fate. It is not that the neoclassical analysis of the market is merely a neutral analysis of the price mechanism that then allows for other disciplines like theology and moral philosophy to determine the sources of value. Quite the contrary! This analysis carries with it a suppressed theology which functions as a quasi-coercive circumcision/baptism. We are grafted into its narrative because it is the only way we have to effect necessary daily exchanges. When we ask for our daily bread, we at the same time find our lives serving this all-ruling providence, whose name we are not sure of. The god of the *agora* (the market)—which seems to be a god of titanic human power—seeks to subvert the God of the church or synagogue. The result will be that whether we like it or not, everything has a formal value, a price—automobiles, food, shelter, clothing, fetal tissue, adoptable children, and even death itself.

SECTION 5
THE PROPRIETY OF MARKET EXCHANGE
NANCY FOX

It appears to be beyond question that everything *can* have a price. What is at issue is whether everything *ought to* have a price. Here is where economics and theology part company. Critics of the market have two concerns. One, that the market system will encroach onto areas where it is not appropriate. "The attempt to sell gift values on the market makes a mockery of those values and subordinates the provider of them" (Anderson, 1990, 188).

> The Chicago school of economics tends to conceive of everything people may value as a scarce commodity with a price . . . policy analysts ask us to make monetized trade-offs about the length

and quality of life in order to allocate health-care resources; they ask us to value life in dollars in order to find out the "right" level of occupational safety risk. Is there anything wrong with reasoning that way? If there are realms of social life that are or should be off-limits to the market, how should we delineate those realms? . . . What (if anything) is wrong with commodification of everything? (Radin, 1996, xii)

She continues: "Systematically conceiving of personal attributes as fungible objects is threatening to personhood, because it detaches from the person that which is integral to the person" (Radin, 1996, 88).

Another concern is that it is impossible for both a market driven value and other driven value to coexist without the market value's taking over and subverting other intrinsic values. Radin describes this phenomenon as the "domino theory."

The domino theory holds that there is a slippery slope leading from toleration of sales of something to an exclusive market regime for that thing, and there is a further slippery slope from a market regime for some things to a market regime encompassing everything people value. The domino theory implicitly makes two claims: . . . it is important for a non-market regime to exist. And a non-market regime cannot coexist with a market regime. The market drives out the non-market version; hence the market regime must be banned. (Radin, 1996, 99)

Radin continues, "Altruism is foreclosed if both sales and donations are permitted. If sales are not allowed, donations have no market value and remain non-monetized. If sales are allowed, then even gifts have a market equivalent" (Radin 1996, 96).

Rose-Ackerman makes the point more concretely:

Why should you sacrifice if others are getting paid to do the same thing? Thus if blood and body parts are purchased from some, donations can be expected to fall. One's feelings of moral obligation may be undermined by the payment of compensation. Instead of feeling under an obligation to take an action or accept a burden without payment, one may feel entitled to a compensation. (Rose-Ackerman, 1998, 3)

Zelizer addresses the market's possible encroachment when she traces the development of money as a gift. The more traditional view that "markets did wipe out the more socially embedded gift exchange" is increasingly challenged by "those who argue that different forms of exchange coexist in modern society" (Zelizer, 1996, 77). Money more or less crept into the gift giving arena in the early twentieth century, first as appropriate in business from superiors to inferiors and then into personal gift exchange. Despite some people's concern that "the same legal tender used to pay salaries, bribe officials . . . [could not] also serve as a sentimental gift that expressed personal care, affection, or joy, monetization of gifts did not deplete social life of meaning, dry up social relations and annul gift exchanges" (Zelizer, 1996, 115). She concludes that "as money entered the sphere of personal gift giving in early twentieth-century America, we have seen that it did not corrupt, or repress people's social exchanges" (Zelizer, 1996, 117).

It is logical to extend this analysis to other arenas where money is deemed an inappropriate medium. Indeed, Rose-Ackerman offers examples where both the market and altruism coexist, apparently without having a negative affect one on the other. Universities that charge $30,000 a year for tuition do not appear to lack generous donations to their endowments. The same can be said for cultural institutions (Rose-Ackerman, 1998, 10).

Giving money is more efficient than giving a gift. Waldfogel estimates that gift giving results in a significant deadweight loss ($4–$38 billion) to society. Despite his empirical results, his survey data reveal that people feel uncomfortable giving money as a gift—while simultaneously acknowledging that they would rather receive cash (Waldfogel, 1998, 78). When a commodity is traded for money, its inherent value is somehow perceived to be diminished. Rose-Ackerman observes that this view is the mirror image of Veblen's. He "claimed that some goods became more valuable to people the higher the price since price was taken as a measure of a goods' social value . . . society attributes moral value to people who spend money on conspicuous consumption" (Rose-Ackerman, 1998, 9).

Critics (such as Marx, Weber, and Simmel, who cut across an entire range of disciplines) allege that "the very essence of money [value in exchange or price] was its unconditional interchangeability, the internal uniformity that makes each piece interchangeable for another" (Zelizer, 1996, 7). They concluded that when value in exchange is used as "the measure of value, . . . the priceless itself surrenders to price" (Zelizer, 1996, 8). Such reasoning misses a main point. The market *measures* value; the market does not create value. A misconception of what economists do was in evidence over a hundred years ago, when Alfred Marshall noted and attempted to clarify it.

> . . . the true philosophic raison d'être of the [economic] theory is that it supplies a machinery to aid us in reasoning about those motives of human action, which are measurable. . . . A misleading association has grown up in people's minds between that measurement of motives, which is the chief task of economic science, and an exclusive regard for material wealth, to the neglect of other and higher objects of desire. The only condition required for a measure for economic purposes is that it should be definite and transferable. (Marshall, 1885, 158)

In "Grounding for the Metaphysics of Morals," Kant made the argument against what would become "universal commodification." "In the kingdom of ends, everything has either a price or a dignity: whatever has a price can be replaced by something else or its equivalent; . . . whatever is above all price . . . and therefore admits of no equivalent, has a dignity."

Centuries later, Elizabeth Anderson clarifies Kant's assertion: "[T]here are two kinds of value, relative worth and intrinsic worth. Everything is either a mere means, with a price or relative value, or an end in itself, with an intrinsic worth which Kant calls 'dignity'" (Anderson, 1993, 9). She distinguishes between market goods and nonmarket goods. The former are appropriately traded in the market, and the latter are not. When the value of a good is measured by its value in exchange in the market, that commodity becomes "something one regards as interchangeable with any other item of the same kind and quality and something that one is prepared to trade with equanimity for any other commodity at some price" (Anderson, 1990, 181). If we do this, we ignore the inherent value of that commodity.

Radin echoes this view: "Universal commodification implies that all value can be expressed in terms of price. For those who believe value is not unitary in this way, commodification reduces all values to sums of money. . . . Commodification is, thus, also a conceptual scheme that is committed to commensurability of value. . . . There is no mystery about which of two items is more valuable; it is the one with the highest price" (Radin, 1996, 8). Here Radin describes the economist's concept of complete preferences: faced with two choices, the consumer either prefers one to another or is indifferent between them. The consumer is assumed to value the option he chooses more than the one he does not, making the two choices de facto commensurable, which Radin defines as "capable of being reduced to money without changing value, and completely interchangeable with every other commodity in terms of exchange value" (Radin, 1996, 3). However, the economist would argue that it is difficult to identify, much less measure, a good's inherent value. Further, the economist's embrace of the concept of individual freedom and determination implies that there is no such thing as inherent value, which would vary from individual to individual.

Anderson levies what might be considered an even harsher criticism of the market. "The market is open to all indifferently, as long as they have the money to pay for the goods. Money income—not one's personal status, characteristics or relationships—is what determines one's access to the real of commodity values" (Anderson, 1990, 181). Curiously, economists view this aspect as one of the market's great strengths: by making access available to all (who have a dollar in their pockets), regardless of status and personal relationship—the market can be viewed as a great equalizer. If all one needs is money to acquire goods, then everyone has a chance in the sense that economic success is not limited by political power or family background.

Organ transplantation provides an excellent illustration. It is well known that there are not enough organs available. In the past few decades, Governor Casey of Pennsylvania received a heart and liver transplant, and Mickey Mantle received a liver transplant. It is difficult to believe that these men did not benefit from their political and social status. This is not to argue that money should be the sole determinant of distribution of this scarce resource, nor to argue that if the organs had been available for a price on the market that Casey and Mantle would not have had an advantage—nonetheless over others—but that the playing field would have been more even if the organs had been available for a price in a legitimate market.

There are some things that are alienable—they can be separated from the person who owns them, and there are some things that are inalienable—they cannot (or should not) be separated from the person who owns them. Goods that are alienable can be traded in the market; they are, or become, commodities. "Inalienability is ascribed to an entitlement, right, or attribute that cannot be voluntarily transferred from one holder to another" (Radin, 1996, 17). Historically, political and civil rights as well as duties, are inalienable; they cannot be traded. A citizen cannot sell his right to vote; a draftee cannot legally buy his way out of military service.[13]

One of the usual arguments in favor of commodification is that the trades which people enter into of their own free will are acceptable. Liberals, says Radin, object to the sale of goods such as body organs, blood, child labor, and babies because "We should presume . . . that such transactions are not the results of free choice" (Radin, 1996, 50). They are sometimes referred to as "trades of last resort." When we ban trades of goods that some believe ought to be inalienable, because sales of such goods "diminish [the sellers] as persons" (Radin, 1996, 50), we are eliminating opportunities for these individuals. "In shutting the valve, society implies that there must be better ways of preventing or alleviating that desperation" (Okun, 1975, 20). Thus, if society bans such trades without providing comparable compensation, it is making those persons worse off than if they were permitted to make the trades.

## Section 6
### Inherent Values
### Steve Long

If the market merely measures value without creating it, then my critique of the neoclassical economists is not valid. My suspicious view of modern economics as predicated on the death of God may still be accepted, but such a loss of God in modernity is not the result of the market. It merely registers for us that theological truths are no longer fashionable. People do not want them. But I do not think this is true. The problem in the modern world is not that people no longer desire theological truths but that theology does not matter. I mean that in the most literal sense. Theology has no flesh, no embodiment in daily existence. Instead, it is forced to the margins of everyday life to some sacred noumenal realm which is neither rational nor irrational. Theology has become the arational. Theology's marginalization is not the result of some malicious conspiracy of economists, business tycoons, or corporate executives. Theology's marginalization was in many respects its own doing. Joseph Schumpeter recognized this best when he argued that:

Capitalist practice turns the unit of money into a tool of rational cost-profit calculations, of which the towering monument is double-entry bookkeeping. Without going into this, we will notice that, primarily a product of the evolution of economic rationality, the cost-profit calculus in turn reacts upon that rationality; by crystallizing and defining numerically, it powerfully propels the logic of enterprise. And thus defined and quantified for the economic sector, this type of logic or attitude or method then starts upon its conqueror's career subjugating—rationalizing—man's tools and philosophies, his medical practice, his picture of the cosmos, his outlook on life, everything in fact including his concepts of beauty and justice and his spiritual ambitions. In this respect it is highly significant that modern mathematico-experimental science developed, in the fifteenth, sixteenth and seventeenth centuries, not only with the social process usually referred to as the Rise of Capitalism, but also outside of the fortress of scholastic thought and in the face of its contemptuous hostility. . . . By cursing it all, scholastic professors in the Italian universities showed more sense than we give them credit for. The trouble was not with individual unorthodox propositions. Any decent schoolman could be trusted to twist his texts so as to fit the Copernican system. But those professors quite rightly sensed the spirit behind such exploits—the spirit of rationalist individualism, the spirit generated by rising capitalism. (Schumpeter, 1975, 123–24)

Schumpeter is wrong in arguing that the rise of a universal mathematics occurred outside fortress scholasticism. In fact, it occurred within it. It was invented by the scholastic philosopher, Descartes. He separated mind from things in the world in an effort to construct a universal mathematics that would allow us to make sense of those things with a clear and certain knowledge. This mathematics became secure separate from any human evaluation. Facts were distinguished from values; and values were utterly separated from the facts themselves. Values became subjective, facts objective.

The result was that terms such as the good, true, and beautiful were rendered subjective whereas the accountant's cost ledger contained the real truth about the world. Beauty disappeared and utility triumphed. This is why economists must argue, as Fox has argued, that "the economist's embrace of the concept of individual freedom and determination implies that there is no such thing as inherent value, which would vary from individual to individual." An individual now looks out on a life-less and form-less world of mathematical facts and can only see them valuable in terms of his or her own will. The beauty of the world disappears, unless it can be conceded by some utility.

As Marx puts it, the capitalist goes for a walk in the forest and thinks "matchsticks." Of course, in such a world, theology will be rendered useless. But such a world cannot sustain itself for long; it is too obviously false.

When economists do question "from whence cometh the source of value," the answer remains epiphenomenal. For instance, take Liebenstein's argument that the "societal determinants of consumer preference" are based on either the "bandwagon" or "snob" effect. But this is merely to state the obvious. People mimic other people, and sometimes in foolish ways. Little girls try to look heroine-chic. Every school kid will soon know and act out the latest Disney movie. Adults likewise fetishize certain goods. That we mimic each other is obvious and does not explain the source of value. The question is why do we do this?

James Alison, drawing on the work of René Girard, has argued that mimetic desire arises from a false sense of individual uniqueness and originality. I want to be unique, but I do so by imitating others. Such imitation betrays the falseness of my own originality. Alison gives the following example:

> If I recognize my absolute dependence on the other for my desire, in both the personal and social sphere, then I am at peace with the other. However, the moment I seek to affirm that my desire is

previous and original, then I'm in a conflictual relationship with the other. A trivial example: a member of my group appears with some new jeans of a certain brand. It's someone I like and admire: I'd like to be like him, if I were like him, then perhaps I'd be more desirable, more attractive, myself. Perhaps I might even "be" a bit more. So, I buy the same jeans, and, of course the others in the group comment, "Look you've imitated Tom, you've bought the same jeans." Now if I were that extraordinarily rare and sane thing, a humble and simple person, I'd reply, "Yes you're right. I like Tom and I'd like to be more like him." However, it's more probable that 99 percent of us would reply: "You're crazy: no way am I imitating him. I saw these jeans in the shop, or on TV, before he even suspected their existence. I just didn't have the money at the time." So I affirm that my desire was previous and original, and I deny my real dependence on the other. (Alison, 1996, 19)

The problem arises when that which gives me my identity is scarce. Then mimetic desire becomes dangerous. If we cannot both have "X," but both of us find our originality and uniqueness in imitation by possessing "X," we must finally fight over "X." Perhaps this can be done by acquisition in the market. Perhaps it is done through violence. Nevertheless, Girard and Alison have shown the superficiality of Liebenstein and Veblen's analysis. Value does not merely arise as a surface phenomenon based on mimetic desire. Those mimetic desires have metaphysical and theological foundations. The question that remains is—if this is correct—what does it mean for the study of economics? Should we think of it as an autonomous discipline that just gives us the facts, or should we imagine it as a traditioned inquiry that requires an underlying, but contingent, politics in order to produce in us the virtues that politics needs to sustain itself? Most importantly of all, what makes a political and economic action rational?

# — 3 —

## WHAT MAKES THEOLOGY "POLITICAL"?

### Come Let Us Reason Together

Nancy Fox and I presented the differences between the ends and first principles of theology and economics. We divided in order to unite but did not do much uniting. This chapter is an essay in practical reasoning that will begin to provide a context within which that uniting might take place. I will not resolve the differences between us but will develop a framework of ad hominem practical reasoning that will point us in a fruitful direction. In so doing, I want to offer a theological account of politics that would assume truth and goodness are more basic than power. If economists and theologians would agree on this, then we might know how to go on. Nevertheless, if this is not acknowledged, I fear the two disciplines could only be mired in an incommensurable conflict.

Earlier I argued that economics could not be construed as a neutral discipline independent of politics and theology. It assumes both. However, how do we make this explicit and how do we assess its reasonableness? This raises the questions, what makes a political and economic action rational? How does theology contribute to such rational action? As we saw in the previous chapter, for Weber *rational* meant congruent with one's own interest. Marginal utility views rational action in terms of value. Does theology escape this when it argues that a rational action is one that orders the agent to his or her true end: friendship with God? Does virtue really differ from value?

Knowledge of God is not a means to any other end; it has no utilitarian value when it is faithfully pursued. It cannot and should not be politicized or used to develop a defense of some economic system. It is intrinsically good, and not good because of its usefulness for something else. Thus it is worthwhile for persons to seek knowledge of God simply because it will help them pray, praise, worship, and adore God well. Theologians seldom find this kind of theology political, it is "fundamental" or "systematic" theology. So be it. If theology must be politically useful, then how could it avoid turning God into an "instrumental value"? Yet, much of contemporary theology insists that it be political. In fact, theologians have produced new forms of theology that were intended to make the political nature of theology more explicit.

Two such modern theological movements have arisen. One is called political theology (and I would place liberation theology within this category) and the other is public theology. So what is present in the theologies that makes them political or public and overcomes a deficiency in other forms of theology? In answering this question, we must remember Oliver O'Donovan's rejoinder that desire to make theology political receives overwhelming positive affirmation in contemporary theology such that it inadvertently depoliticizes theology altogether. When even how we name God is a matter of virulent political contestation, rational human action has been construed on Weberian grounds—how does this name fit with my own assertion of power? If that is all we mean by a political theology, then we will not escape the Weberian first principles that define so much of both economics and contemporary Christian theology.

Before theologians claim the term *political* for their work, perhaps some consideration as to the assumptions behind a political and an apolitical theology are in order. Few theologians these days would claim their work is apolitical, yet theologians regularly accuse others of producing such a theology, which has become a decisive objection to a theology's adequacy. In fact, types of theology have emerged based on the assumption that their difference from other theologies is their *political* cast. Liberation and public theologies, different in many respects, would not make sense without the common tacit background assumption that other theologies fail to be political, or at least adequately political, and their work corrects this defect. These "political" theologies often position other theologies via this tacit background assumption. They accomplish this by categorizing the apolitical or inadequately political theologies as "church" theology, or as sectarian, fideist, or ideological. Thus, we are caught in an interminable conflict between those who claim their theology is "political" while suggesting others are "ideological" or "ecclesia" theology.[14] We seem to be at a stalemate in this debate. Is it possible to advance the argument?

To do so requires addressing the question: what makes a theological work political, apolitical, or inadequately political? I do not think an answer to this question can be found in the material production of theological works themselves. All theological *works* share a similar "social location" in relation to contemporary political and economic institutions, and this poses a particular difficulty for liberation theologians who tell us their work has overcome ideology or false consciousness and offer a material practice other theologies ignore. We all seem to produce theological works through roughly the same means.[15] We sit before computers and type, or put pen and pencil to paper, craft arguments, and seek publication for them through publishing houses or journals. Some works might then bear the title "political, liberation, or public" theology, but the concrete material reality of the work cannot render one political and another apolitical, one public and another sectarian, one material and another ideological. I cannot distinguish the books in my library based on their political or apolitical character solely on their material reality. What then does distinguish them? Is it the social location of the author, the sources drawn upon, or the content of the argument?

Each of these three possibilities is theologically significant, but a little reflection proves none of them decisive in claiming the adjective "political" for a theology. The diverse social locations of authors provide different "takes on" the world, but no clear correlation between one's class, gender, ethnicity, or social location and one's political theology can be made. Too much theological variety among similar social locations, and too much theological similarity among different social locations, exists for anyone to claim too much for social location itself. Counter factual arguments are readily available. When such arguments for social location are made too encompassing, they quickly become unsupportable.

Likewise, the sources drawn upon make a difference, but again no clear correlation between sources and politics can be secured. Analyzing tortured victims' testimonies or comparing Thomas Aquinas and Gregory Palamas produce different theologies, but that does not mean that one will necessarily be political and the other apolitical. So perhaps it is finally the content of the argument itself that determines whether theology is political or not? Some people write on ideas and others write on material practices? However, this only shifts the question, for who decides what constitutes a political content and what becomes a mere "history of ideas" since both are presented through the same material means? Who decides what makes one theology sectarian or ecclesial and another political or public? And, of course, the answer is no one decides—for a final decision cannot be made.

The debate among the various opponents of political, public, and "church" theology cannot be decided through apodictic means; it cannot even be advanced in those terms. If we could easily correlate specific material productions or race, class, gender, and ethnicity to specific takes on political theology, then the debate could be settled with apodictic certainty. We could have a table where the publication, or the authors' social location, or the sources cited could be indexed to specific politics. All we would then need to do is use that table as a scientist uses the periodic chart of the elements in order to determine the politics of each theological work. Of course, that is both impossible and foolish, even though some of the claims for "social location" these days approach claiming that kind of apodictic certainty. Whether or not theology is political, or adequately political, is not a function of that kind of scientific reasoning. It can only be a function of practical reasoning. It alone can advance the argument. The best we can do to adjudicate these differences is to engage in, as Charles Taylor has so aptly put it, practical ad hominem arguments.

### PRACTICAL AD HOMINEM ARGUMENTS

The difference between those who claim their theology is political or public and others' theology is sectarian or ideological does not need to remain at a stalemate. The differences between these theological camps can be adjudicated by drawing on Charles Taylor's understanding of practical reasoning. Taylor distinguishes two models of practical reasoning: apodictic and ad hominem (Taylor, 1995, 34). Apodictic practical reasoning assumes opponents' fundamental first premises vary so radically that they cannot reason together. We can only reason together if our opponents come to adopt a completely different first premise—the ones we hold. Thus, apodictic practical reasoning assumes a stark contrast when comparing first premises, either complete translatability or incommensurability. If this is the assumption when we compare theology and economics, then we would be unable to advance the argument.

Ad hominem practical reasoning does not assume that stark contrast; it assumes "my opponent already shares at least some of the fundamental dispositions toward good and right which guide me." Reasoning within these shared dispositions permits me to argue "the error" of my opponent "comes from confusion, unclarity, or an unwillingness to face some of what he can't lucidly repudiate" (Taylor, 1995, 36). This is the kind of practical reasoning Fox and I were tacitly engaging in throughout our conversation; we assumed the context of the good and the true even when it was not always made explicit. Without this, no reason exists for the conversation. Apodictic practical reasoning tempts us because designating first premises as incommensurable leaves us free from confronting the implicit errors in our positions given our shared disposition. By articulating what is merely implicit in my opponent's position, and showing how it conflicts with our shared dispositions, a "transition" can occur whereby the opponent comes to see that he cannot practically adhere to his old characterization of my position without violating that shared disposition. Of course, that transition might also occur with me coming to realize the same thing; ad hominem practical reasoning assumes an openness to conversion for reasoning to occur.

In the question at hand, our shared disposition is that "theology should be political or public." I think most theologians share this basic premise. (This does not mean everything is political.) Therefore, if my opponent begins by assuming that my theology is sectarian or ideological, he advocates an apodictic form of practical reasoning, which is simply another version of the "sectarian" position with which he seeks to tar me. In other words, his argument goes like this. Theology should be political and public. It should not assume some fideistic first principle that refuses critical reasoning from outside its own enclave. Those sectarian and ideologically driven theologians cannot be reasoned with because they do not share my first principle. However, this is self-refuting and it begs the question. It refuses to address the fact that those of us called sectarian and ideological never claimed an apodictic practical reasoning in the first place. We have never clung to a first principle incapable of critical scrutiny from outside its enclave. We simply argue that theology cannot adopt a position from nowhere. It is always already situated in a politics and a public, and no single politics or public exists. If political or public theologians continue this charge against us, they assume an apodictic practical reasoning in order to charge us with it. They are the ones who refuse the charitable disposition of reasoning together.

Theology should be political. On this, we agree; we share a fundamental disposition. Given what we know at the present moment, whether it is or is not political cannot be determined solely based on the material production of theological works, the social location of authors, the sources used, or the content of the argument. No argument has yet been set forth for the political character of theology solely linked to these concepts or practices that is so persuasive it cannot easily be challenged with a counterfactual argument. No "periodic chart of political theology" yet exists. Ad hominem practical reasoning helps us enter into the argument and move it beyond the stalemate of assertion and counterassertion by recognizing that those who would charge others with being sectarian or ideological, rather than political or public, must themselves adopt an apodictic practical reasoning where first principles are posited to be so incommensurable that they a priori distinguish apolitical from political, or sectarian (private) from public, and refuse practical reasoning with the other position. These distinctions collapse under the very conditions necessary to uphold them. Theology cannot claim to be political or public against other non-political or sectarian theologies without adopting the posture of apodictic practical reasoning. That violates the very heart of ad hominem practical reasoning, where we do not begin with the stark either-or of radical incommensurability or complete translatability.

## WHAT CONSTITUTES A RATIONAL POLITICAL ACTION?

To assume that our alternatives are either radical incommensurability or complete translatability is to begin at the wrong place. Ad hominem practical reasoning assumes the virtues of charity, generosity, and hospitality. We assume that we can "reason together," but that does not mean we assume perfect agreement. To say we share a disposition provides a basis for argument, but it does not entail complete agreement on what constitutes politics. Our shared disposition opens up a conversation; it does not end it. It assumes that all human activity takes place under the pursuit of goodness, apparent or real. Theology should be political, and at some level politics has to do with human flourishing. This means that we seek what is good for our neighbors near and far. I cannot imagine a theologian working today who would not consent to this even though it does not yet say much. However, I shall argue that a variation on the term *politics* has crept into some forms of liberation and public theology where this broad, ill-defined concept of politics we share cannot be adequately sustained. This came about primarily through the influence of Max Weber's account of what constitutes a rational political action, its hold on the social sciences, and the adoption of those sciences by theologians. Here we see evidence of the encroaching logic of the market on theology.

Weber's work can only produce apodictic practical reasoning because it assumes "thin, nomothetic" statements of discrete types of human action. This means that a simple, law-like account of action can be independent of its context within a richer, narrative whole. For instance, Weber decisively distinguished economic from political action based on such a simple law-like account of action. "Economic action," he stated, "is any peaceful exercise of an actor's control over resources which is in its main impulse oriented toward economic ends. Rational economic action requires instrumental rationality in this orientation, that is deliberate planning" (Weber, 1978, 63). Note that Weber understands economic action as instrumental and nonviolent. This contrasts with his understanding of rational political action. It differs from economic action precisely in its relation to violence, which is for him the "decisive political means."

In his famous essay, "Politics as a vocation," Weber relates ethics and politics. He divides ethics into an "ethics of responsibility" and an "ethics of ultimate ends." Only the former can be political for only it requires "one to give an account of the foreseeable results of one's actions." Like economic action, it must be instrumental; thus, both rational economic and political actions are a *kind* of practical reasoning. This contrasts with his description of an ethics of ultimate ends. It refuses this instrumental account of action, and, thus, refuses practical reasoning. It is the ethic of the "chiliastic prophet" who seeks to live by Christ's Sermon on the Mount without attending to its practical consequences. However, this person, whom Troeltsch made infamous with his category *sectarian*, cannot live consistently with his desire to refuse to give an account of the foreseeable results of his actions. For this reason, the ethics of ultimate ends is dangerous. It is an impractical ethics. Yet, what kind of practical reasoning does Weber assume here? He sets these two ethics in opposition because of incommensurable first premises. Then he tells us that only an ethics of responsibility can engage in practical reasoning, for only it attends to consequences of actions. This is apodictic practical reasoning. It does not assume a shared disposition toward the good of neighbors near and far, and Weber is explicit about this. It assumes that violence and conflict alone provide the foundation on which practical reasoning can occur.

The practical reasoning entailed in an ethics of responsibility recognizes two correlative claims. First, it recognizes that not every other person shares a common disposition toward the good. To assume otherwise is a dangerous element of the "ethics of ultimate ends." Weber writes, "a man who believes in an ethic of responsibility takes account of precisely the average deficiencies of people; as Fichte has correctly said, he does not even have the right to presuppose their goodness and perfection." Weber's ethics cannot adopt ad hominem practical reasoning because he assumes the apodictic stance that persons meet with fundamentally opposed dispositions. Either they have an ethics of ultimate ends or they have an ethics of responsibility. The two ethics cannot begin to reason together. The result, of course, is that people are not drawn together politically by goodness or truth, they are primarily drawn together by power and incommensurable interests. Therefore, the second correlative claim for this kind of practical reasoning is that "the decisive means for politics is violence" (Weber, 1958, 120–21). It is not always used, but it is always present. Its presence alone makes action political rather than economic. Both calculate foreseeable consequences, but one does so without assuming the use of violence and the other does so always within the context of violence—within the recognition that my neighbor cannot be, and should not be, trusted.

Given the hold of the social sciences on theology, and the recurring call for an adequate analysis of power in theology, it comes as no surprise that to offer a political analysis too often requires beginning where Weber began. It requires a power analysis of competing interests in specific contexts always under the threat of violence. It is a priori assumed in much of liberation and public theology that any persons who do not begin with this fundamental law of politics cannot adequately produce political theology. Because these nomothetic descriptions appear to be universal, neutral descriptions of rational economic and political action, they rule out reasoning practically with those who cannot share this fundamental premise. They will be dismissed as apolitical, sectarian, ideological. The irony is that those who issue these dismissals must have adopted the very enclave reality they seek to avoid in order to attribute it to their opponents. Others must adopt the first principle of Weber's political ethics if they are allowed into the conversation.

Weber's work has had a decisive influence on political and public theologies. Theological critiques that position others' theologies as apolitical because they lack a power analysis easily fall prey to the Weberian take on the political. Think how odd it would be for those in this tradition if someone argued a theology was inadequately political because it lacked an analysis of truth or goodness, which many theologies today clearly lack. It is the power analysis alone that makes theology political, and that requires an insatiable suspicion of any doctrinal claims for truth. This is so common it hardly is recognized. For instance, in his *God and the Excluded,* Rieger runs through contemporary theologies asking what role the excluded have in these theologies. All are found wanting, including radical orthodoxy and postliberal theology. He notes, "Orthodox doctrines, for example, that are thought to reach their referent, also establish a basic identity between God and humanity which can lead to humanity controlling God. Lindbeck does not appear to see much of a problem in the claims of identity as such." However, what is the logical conclusion of this kind of suspicion toward any truthful historical representation of theological conceptions? It means theology cannot be done at all. All theological statements are placed under suspicion as "easily leading to the legitimation of structures which are not ultimate" (Rieger, 2001, 79–80). It is no surprise then that Rieger's political theology does not adequately develop Christian doctrines or see them as politically significant. Theology primarily offers critique, unmasking suspicious linkages between theological and political positions. I think this is a necessary feature of an apodictic practical reasoning where the assumed first premise for political activity is something like Weber's premise.

Gustavo Gutiérrez' definition of politics draws, not on Marx but Weber, when he tells us "the building of a just society means the confrontation—in which different kinds of violence are present between groups with different interests and opinions" (Gutiérrez, 1993, 31). This seems to confirm Alasdair MacIntyre's suspicion that the contemporary worldview even among Marxists remains Weberian. MacIntyre stated, "as Marxists organize and move toward power they always do and have become Weberians in substance, even if they remain Marxists in rhetoric; for in our culture we know of no organized movements towards power which is not bureaucratic and managerial in mode and we know of no justifications for authority which are not Weberian in form" (MacIntyre, 1984, 109).

Consistent calls for, and criticisms of, others based solely on "power analysis" repeats that Weberian form. If political bonds are primarily "different kinds of violence," then the best we can do is manage them. Any claims to truth or goodness can only be treated with suspicion. Given Weber's hold on the social sciences and their adoption by theologians it comes as no surprise that a political or adequately political theology must assume persons meet not desiring goodness or truth, but under the always potentially violent conflict of incommensurate interests and conflicting desires for power.[16] If this is the case, no ad hominem practical reasoning is possible. Political theology will only begin when this thin, nomothetic first premise is adopted. All who reject it will appear to those who accept it as sectarian, ideological or churchy, and incapable of reason. Thus, they are finally dismissed as "fideists."

Weber's tradition of rational political action, violence and democracy explains why the modern liberal nation-state needs war to be political. Max Weber provided one of the most influential conceptions of how the term politics functions in modern life. This conception has a lasting influence on how persons relate theology and politics, for Ernst Troeltsch mediated it to the discipline of "Christian Ethics" through his profound historical narration of the church's social teachings. Reinhold Niebuhr drew on this analysis to set in place the apodictic conditions by which theology could be political. From the publication of his *Moral Man and Immoral Society* in 1932 until his death in 1971, he was, without a doubt, the most influential voice in Protestant Christian social ethics. Niebuhr's theology fits well the Weberian tradition for it assumes that politics is fundamentally an analysis of competing claims to power, always within the context of violence, which goes by the name realism. It too is a form of apodictic practical reasoning. "Realism," he states, "denotes the disposition to take all factors in a social and political situation, which offers resistance to established norms, into account, particularly the factors of self-interest and power" (Niebuhr, 1977, 119). To be political, one must adopt this disposition; but this is pure Weberianism. Niebuhr, like the tradition of the social sciences, subordinates truth and goodness to power. Only an analysis of the latter constitutes politics. Any commitment to truth or goodness brings with it the unintended consequences—whereby living out of one's commitment to truth or goodness is more dangerous than holding all commitments loosely, recognizing that they are all inevitably distorted by power.

Because self-interest and power are inextricably present in every exchange, no unalloyed true, good, and loving deed is possible. For Niebuhr, to hold to such a possibility in politics is dangerous. It denies our most basic being, both individually and socially, and prevents an adequate political analysis of the ineradicable element of self-interest and power by putting forth the possibility of an exchange where perversion is not always already present. For this reason, he found Catholicism, in particular, quite dangerous. "The Catholic doctrine of the Church," he wrote, "is in fact a constant temptation to demonic pretensions, since it claims for an institution, established in time and history, universal and absolute validity" (Niebuhr, 1963, 143). But notice how Niebuhr's Weberian politics functions apodictically, and notice its similarity to Rieger's argument. We know—without argument—that any institution in history (and what other kinds are there) that claims to be grounded in truth is a priori "demonic," sacrificing the ultimate for the historical and penultimate.[17] For the same reason Niebuhr could not countenance the Anabaptists or the Wesleyans as offering an adequate political theology. Like Weber, Niebuhr assumed these three ecclesial traditions were filled with false consciousness because they adhered to an ethics of ultimate ends and were, thus, incapable of practical reasoning. They are fideists before the conversation begins.

Niebuhr knew a priori that politics was the negotiation of incommensurable elements. He wrote, "To understand life in its total dimension means contrition because every moral achievement stands under the criticism of a more essential goodness.

If fully analyzed the moral achievement is not only convicted of imperfection, but of sin. It is not only wanting in perfect goodness, but there is something of the perversity of evil in it" (Niebuhr, 1977, 52). The first part of this quote is promising. Here life occurs for Niebuhr under the pursuit of "a more essential goodness," but unfortunately that goodness can only function negatively. It can never be embodied. It only stands over and against us. Its negative function is even more than that of a regulative ideal. We do not merely want perfect goodness (a claim even this Wesleyan is willing to concede); every human act is mired in a "perversity of evil." As with Weber, so with Niebuhr, this rules out ad hominem practical reasoning. We cannot reason together, for I cannot assume you and I share a disposition toward the good and the true. The moment I make such an assumption, I lose the necessary critical distance by which I can stand in judgment over the incommensurable power differential in every political exchange.

Niebuhr's theology works well both as a legitimation for modern political and economic arrangements and as means for critiquing them, which is how they are legitimated; for they themselves are not based on any commitment to truth or goodness. They assume the best political arrangements are those that recognize that power is more determinative than either truth or goodness as the bonds that can bring people together and, thus, what legitimates them is that they are always subject to critique and protest. Although a federalist republic like the United States of America was forged against an original "predominant and excessive zeal for liberty," that worried the framers of the Constitution. It was still dependent solely on the principle that attention to self-interest, self-deceit and power should be more determinative of our politics than truth or goodness.[18] As Alexander Hamilton wrote in the *Federalist Papers*, "Is it now time to awake from the deceitful dream of a golden age and to adopt as a practical maxim for the direction of our political conduct that we, as well as the other inhabitants of the globe are yet remote from the happy empire of perfect wisdom and perfect virtue?" The violence of the U.S. enterprise over the last two centuries has certainly proven Hamilton correct. We received the politics we sought.

The common fear that one group might aggrandize itself against the others in its efforts to be that "happy empire" prompts both the necessity and the possibility of a political union. It is forged, not out of strength or truth, but out of "common weakness."[19] Niebuhr's theology safeguards this insight. As he wrote in *Children of Light and Children of Darkness*, "Man's capacity for justice makes democracy possible; but man's inclination to injustice makes democracy necessary." All of life—political, social, theological—is a balance of power, a calculation of interests dominated by self-interest, and power dynamics that make any exchange possible. The best we can do is counteract one self-interest with another so that none becomes absolute and destroys us all. Liberal politics is the ontologization of incommensurability and, thus, it can only reason apodictically.

## WHY NOT GOODNESS AND TRUTH?

Weber and Niebuhr's apodictic understanding of politics seduces its adherents to sectarianism in that it tempts them to guard a first premise as to what constitutes "politics" and rules out of the conversation any who refuse this basic premise. Its adherents cannot engage in ad hominem practical reasoning with those who do not define politics primarily in terms of contending power interests. This rules out the tradition of politics in Aristotle and Plato. It rules out the political theology of Augustine and Aquinas. It rules out much of the Catholic, Anabaptist, and Wesleyan traditions. They must adopt Weber and Niebuhr's (neo-Protestant) first premise or be relegated to the status of apolitical, sectarian, and ideological.

Theology is apolitical if it refuses to take into account power in specific contexts, but such an analysis cannot define politics without remainder or there can be no true politics. If power analysis primarily defines the political without reference to truth or goodness, then several problems emerge. First, it perpetuates the assumption that bonds of human solidarity do not actually exist. If all that brings us together is a competition for power, no politics can emerge. No city truly functions without a priority to peace and cooperation assuming basic shared goods. Second, once politics is understood in these Weberian terms, the only political task will be to unmask and disclose ad nauseam the power differential in every exchange. The term political will be reduced to the status given it by evening news reporters when they tell us that the President's speech was political. By that, they do not mean it was seeking truth and the good of neighbors near and far; they mean it was an exercise in manipulation. Third, those who adopt this account of the political must assume their own innocent relations to the power differential in order to expose its ideological use in others. Finally, this prevents the ongoing task of ad hominem practical reasoning where something more than assertion and counter-assertion can emerge. It prevents us from reasoning together.

I do not assume Rieger's, Gutiérrez', and Niebuhr's followers define politics solely in terms of power. "Sectarianism" is impossible. I assume they also think politics proceeds under the pursuit of some good and entails truth claims. If they are to engage with us in practical reasoning together, they owe us some exemplification of those truth claims. They should tell us their doctrines. We can practically reason together when they refrain from making apodictic criticisms about the relationship between politics and power that refuses to think of it in terms of goodness and truth. That entails a lack of the virtues of charity, hospitality, and generosity which ad hominem practical reasoning requires; these are virtues that the Anabaptist theologian John Howard Yoder embodied in his theological work.

### Practically Reasoning with John Howard Yoder

Yoder was able to stand firmly anchored in his Mennonite tradition and carry on conversations with Protestants, Catholics, Jews, and others with a generosity and hospitality few in the Weberian tradition can countenance. This should be the model for how theology and economics can proceed. Yoder was able to do this because he did not assume every political exchange was primarily a contest of power. As Stanley Hauerwas argued in his Gifford lectures, Yoder begins with the assumption that Christians cannot do political theology without beginning with the truth they receive in the life, death, and resurrection of Jesus Christ. To do otherwise would not be to do Christian political theology, which should be an uncontroversial claim, but it has become highly controversial. This worries many people, for they can only hear an outmoded form of theocratic politics in such a beginning point. However, this overlooks the actual performance of a theologian like Yoder who did not defend the cold war, military intervention, and the pentagon in the same way Niebuhr and the Weberian tradition inevitably did and still do. Yoder never claimed his political theology was sectarian and only for an enclave. He made the daring thesis that he was doing theology "with the grain of the universe." It was his assumption that he was truly engaged with God's politics that led him to an openness to the other, to a charitable reception of diverse theological and faith perspectives. His politics was a politics of human flourishing that sought the good for neighbors near and far. It did not begin with an apodictic assumption of incommensurability where each person or tradition was defined by his, her, or its pursuit of power.

Yoder's political theology requires a different kind of conversation than the one that normally occurs across traditions; for as he noted the usual conversation is not much of a conversation at all. It usually takes place at the liberal edges of the various traditions where the participants "were relatively least bound to the classical core of their respective traditions." That conversation begins by bracketing truth claims and finding common agreement a priori. This is how he explained Reinhold Niebuhr's efforts at interfaith dialogue. Yoder did not reject the conversation occurring at the liberal edges of these various traditions. He wrote, "I rejoice in the refinement of the dialogue already going on between the liberal edges of the [Christian and Jewish] communities, but it is not something to which I have anything to add." The reason Yoder had nothing to add to this conversation was because he did not enter into the conversation from the "liberal margin" but "from the center of Christian identity" (Yoder, 2003, 34). He was no sectarian, but neither did he assume perfect translatability of first premises.

Is it possible to engage others politically without assuming either a complete translatability of our fundamental dispositions or a radical incommensurability? Can we have a politics that works with such an assumption? This is the challenge John Howard Yoder offers.

It would be a politics that comes from the centers of our various identities without apology, but still has place for others because we recognize, from the center of our identity, a common desire that cannot escape truth and goodness. Thus, it would assume that the conversation occurs under the pull of what is good and true in our lives, even when we differ on how we explain that goodness and truth. It would assume that our first political task is to give an account of that truth and its goodness, and then expect the same from others. Any who cannot give such an account are to be pitied, for all they have is power. Unlike Weber and Niebuhr's rational political action that always requires a critical distance from those identities, Yoder embraces them. Weber and Niebuhr subordinate truth and goodness to power for they are convinced that the alternative is too dangerous. If we begin by assuming our identities are true and good, then we will miss the elements of power and self-interest that distort every conception of truth and goodness. The difficulty is that this position gets the politics it deserves.

Yoder begins with the truth of his own identity; he seems untroubled by self-interest. Of course, we have self-interest in our own identities. Otherwise, we would not have those identities, but we would adopt others. Weber and Niebuhr assume Kant's disinterested posture toward our own histories and traditions. Yoder knows he cannot afford that kind of disinterestedness for it would be the foregoing of one identity (Anabaptist Christian) for another (liberal Protestant.) He does not assume that the latter is neutral and universal. Because he is anchored in his history of the Anabaptist tradition, he can see that any adoption of the first premises of the political in Weber and Niebuhr's terms would lead to a conversion from Anabaptism to liberal Protestantism. He listens carefully enough to them that he recognizes this would be required, but he was not persuaded to convert. Therefore, Yoder produced his theological work from the center of his identity without apology.

What is striking in this move is how it surprises persons ensconced in the Weberian tradition. Far from producing an intolerant, inhospitable politics grounded in self-deception, Yoder's work shows that one can begin here, subordinate questions of power to truthful identities, and still have place for others, still practice the virtue of liberality or generosity.

I conclude by making three points that I hope can help us move beyond the current stalemate among public, liberation, and church theologians by adopting Taylor's ad hominem practical reasoning and Yoder's performance of it. I think this has significant implications for how we not only have inter-faith conversation but also speak across disciplines. First, Yoder's politics is less open to violence, force, and coercion of the other than the "ethics of responsibility" set forth by Weber and Niebuhr. This is because the truthfulness of his convictions entails peaceable relations with others. The Weber-Niebuhr tradition assumes an ontological violence where strife and conflict are the norm. Politics is then built upon that ontology. Yoder argues that truth matters; every truth claim is not simply a veiled power move that needs unmasking. It is the latter assumption that must, of necessity, assume a violent politics. Likewise, no economics can avoid the question of truth and goodness. If it has not given us an account of it, it has not yet offered a compelling account of human action. Second, Yoder's position makes possible a more substantive interfaith conversation than that which normally occurs at the liberal margins of traditions. This can be seen in the excellent collection of essays Yoder was working on toward the end of his life which has recently been published entitled *The Christian-Jewish Schism Revisited.* They are brilliant exercises in ad hominem practical reasoning. They begin assuming that our divisions, although real, "do not necessarily have to be." We do not need a politics that secures us from each other's truth claims; we can dare to create a politics where Jews speak as Jews and Christians speak as Christians and still reason together. Fox and I tried to do this in our conversation not so much as a Jew and a Christian, but as an economist and a theologian. Third, Yoder allows for an ad hominem practical rationality in a way Weber and Niebuhr would. I would argue that it is because of his different understanding of politics that these three advances over the Weberian-Niebuhrian tradition are possible. It should help us chart a future conversation for a true political theology. This richer understanding of politics denies that politics is only the distribution of scarce resources, and in this case, power. While that is, of course, one feature of politics, it is a surface and not a depth feature. Likewise, economics does deal with the allocation of scarce resources, and this should not be denied. However, is there not a depth reality to economics that is something other than this? Tripp York and I will try to provide such an account of economics in the concluding chapter.

In his *Body Politics*, Yoder offered an account of politics that is open to others for it refuses a single, apodictic rendering of "political." He begins by recognizing the problem with which my essay began. He states, "There seems to be no end of debating about how the church should or should not be involved in politics" (Yoder, 1994, vi). He then critiques any easy church/politics distinction, but without arguing that the church should be involved in politics for that merely perpetuates the distinction. For Yoder, the church is a politics. He writes, "This study will pick up the topic of the church as body, for its own sake, from the beginning. The Christian community, like any community held together by commitment to important values is a political reality. That is, the church has the character of a polis (the Greek word from which we get the adjective political), namely a structured social body. It has its way of making decisions, defining membership, and carrying out common tasks. That makes the Christian community a political entity in the simplest meaning of the term" (Yoder, 1994, viii). The church is a politics, to ask it to be involved in politics is to ask to adopt an alien first premise. However, it is a politics like other communities based on truthful convictions about the good life, which are also politics. To begin practically reasoning from the perspective of the church as politics requires a reciprocal intentionality to other such communities. We can reason together without requiring everyone to abstract from their commitment to truth and goodness by some apodictically certain and unexceptionable first principle incommensurate with such communities.

In such a politics, terms like *sectarian*, *fideist*, and *ideological* disappear; they will be recognized as terms that only emerge when apodictic practical reasoning takes place. Ad hominem practical reasoning does not mean we refuse to be anchored in our community of truthful convictions. As Yoder put it, "Stated very formally, the pattern we shall discover is that the will of God for human socialness as a whole is prefigured by the shape to which the Body of Christ is called" (Yoder, 1994, ix). For those in the Weberian-Nieburhian tradition the latter will seem arrogant, but it is less so than an apodictic understanding of politics. As already noted, it begins with certainty as to the relationship between politics, power, and violence. Yoder begins with the assumption that the church is the shape of God's politics, and as such it is a pattern based on goodness and truth that might be found in other political societies; for Yoder does not assume a single unitary politics under which everything must fit. This is what makes possible his ad hominem practical reasoning. Moreover, this is why it should form the basis for the next step in the current debates about what makes theology political, including how we might develop a theological economics. It does not decisively answer the question what makes for this politics, but it provides the possibility that we can say to others "come let us reason together" without negating or bracketing out who "we" are in our reasoning.[20]

# — 4 —

## THE THEOLOGY OF ECONOMICS
## Adam Smith as "Church" Father

Now that we have developed an account of ad hominem practical reasoning, I want to use it to argue theologically with the founding father of modern economics, Adam Smith. The neoclassical liberal tradition that originated from his work certainly seeks the good; it is not some unregenerate form of evil that only desires to produce some hegemonic empire. In fact, Smith's theological economics sought the exact opposite of this. However, the role for God in his theological economics is problematic. By recounting the history of the development of my own concern for a theological economics, I hope to show how Smith's theology and ethics cannot account for the common pull toward the good we all desire. It cannot account adequately for the church's teaching on economics. For this reason, Smith should be recognized as a church father of a very different kind of church.

## LEARNING ECONOMICS

My quest to think about, address, and understand the relationship between theology and economics began when I found myself as a local pastor in Honduras in the Caribbean Council of the Methodist churches. I had never read Marx, Adam Smith, or any economic textbook. I had no clue how value was produced nor about the philosophical and social scientific debates as to how it was produced. But many evenings I would give the Guarifuna women who worked at the local lobster and shrimp plant a ride by boat over to the church on the island where I preached. I heard them pray, sing, and talk about work. I saw the conditions under which they worked as we all prepared to worship Jesus together. I could not help but see their work and labor in terms of our common life as Methodist Christians, singing, praying, and preaching long into the evening at least four times a week.

Their work, as was that of their husbands, was demanding. They showed up when the lobster and shrimp boats arrived—boats where many of their husbands worked. Then they started preparing the shrimp and lobster as a commodity for a global market. Of course, while that commodity received its value on a global market, the value of their labor was determined locally. They received approximately seventy cents per hour, which was the best wage on the island (it was basically the only wage on the island). They had no pension, no health care, and no possibility of a trade union—which would have done absolutely no good anyway. They worked when there was work and as long as there was work. After a week's work they were unable to buy the lobster and shrimp from their own waters (and those off the coast of Nicaragua that the shrimp and lobster boats "invaded" to their own peril) that was then sent to land-locked people to be enjoyed at fast-food restaurants as a hobby. Our ride in a boat after a long day's work led me to think what Jesus would say to these women.

Some theologians, pastors, Christian businessmen and women, economists, and social-scientists justify these practices as just the way the world is. It is necessary, perhaps as a result of sin—where we all must labor for our daily bread. But it seemed like some were laboring a whole lot more for a whole lot less, with some "paying" a great deal more for sin than others. This led me to question: is it true this is just the way the world is? Is it natural that some people must labor like this so that others live well? Or is this the result of human making? James K. Smith reminds us of this same question in his wonderful book, *Introducing Radical Orthodoxy*, by drawing on the movie *The Mission*. After a terrible slaughter of the innocent, a cardinal weeps. The Portuguese governor consoles him saying, "We are in the world; the world is thus." But the cardinal replies, "Thus have we made the world. Thus have I *made* it" (Smith, 2004, 196n33). The question is an ontological one—to what extent is economics natural and to what extent is it a matter of *poetics*? To what extent is it a brute *factum* where that word fact has lost its association with the verb *facere* (to make)? I should have not had to go to Honduras to face this question. I should have seen it in the everyday life of the people around me, especially my grandmother who worked thirty-five years in a factory at minimum wage, retired without a pension, and lived only on social security, Medicare, and what her children provided for her. However, for some reason, it took those women in Honduras singing, praying, and talking to raise this question.

I honestly do not know the answer to this question, and I am sure there is not one answer. I think all we can do to address it is present ad hominem practical reasons. I recognize that some well-intended policies do produce more harm than good. But I disagree with Smith's stoicism that good can best emerge from intentionally not intending good. For thus God has not made the world. Nevertheless, I began a quest to understand how economics works, a quest at which I was thoroughly unsuccessful—as most of my economist friends remind me. I began reading from Smith onward through the history of political economy and into economics. I was looking for an answer to the question of how value is produced and if it requires economic practices like those that I saw in Honduras. What I discovered was that there is no unequivocal answer to that question. There was no secret knowledge a group of experts had which , beyond doubt, knew how value was produced.

I discovered that economics was not a science that gave you exact determinations of how value is produced, but a historical tradition that argued over those determinations. John Maynard Keynes helped me see this most of all. He recognized that economics is a moral science; it is about human action that is radically unpredictable. We will never have a "value-producing-machine" whereby we plug in all the data and then receive unequivocally the answer to how we can maximize value or produce the best of all possible economic worlds. There is no objective standpoint, let alone Smith's impartial spectator, who offers a view from above the incalculable aspects of daily exchanges. Nevertheless, this led me to conclude that economics is more like theology than the chemistry I had studied in college. Certain dogmas had to be adopted before one could get into the discipline.

As a Christian theologian, I found that I simply could not accept those dogmas because they conflicted with too much of the Christian tradition. In fact, it became clearer to me that the global market was more like a simulacrum of the Catholic church offering an eschatological, albeit thoroughly stoic, hope rather than a neutral mechanism of exchange. It proclaims to us that if we adopt these dogmas, the streets will be paved with gold; we will have "the wealth of nations."

I was confirmed in this sentiment when I came across the works of Robert Nelson and Michael Budde. Nelson's forthrightness about how the market replaced the church as the institution to which we look for salvation, and his positive appraisal of it in his *Reaching for Heaven on Earth*, along with Buddes' compelling but negative appraisal of the same reality in his *The Two Churches*, led me to abandon my failed attempt to read theology from the perspective of what the economists had to say (that old correlational theology that was still in my soul) and instead to read economists as theologians. I began trying to do this before I read John Milbank's *Theology and Social Theory*, but that work was invaluable in showing me how not to read the social scientists. Social scientists were not theologically neutral; to accept them outside of theology is simply to fail to acknowledge the theological conditions for the possibility of their work.

### ADAM SMITH'S VISION

Thus I began to think of Adam Smith more like a church father of this simulacrum of the church than as a social scientist. If we think of Smith as a church father, and read him as we would read any church father, then we will make better head-way in thinking theologically about economics. This, by no means, is to read Smith negatively, or ironically. Smith is, like Shaftesbury (Anthony Ashley Cooper) a fascinating character who offers us a practical reason rather than an objective theoretical science. My argument does not deny the form of Smith's argument, but seeks to counter it on similar terms. And there is much in Smith to be affirmed, even though his legacy is as contested as that of Thomas Aquinas. (We could easily speak of transcendental Smithians, revisionist Smithians, scholastic Smithians, etc.)

I find the best and most interesting development of Smith as "market" father is Samuel Fleischacker's *On Adam Smith's Wealth of Nations*. He begins his analysis of Smith by reminding us of Smith's imaginative economic vision centered on the role of a pin-making factory. Far from seeing the factory and by implication large multinational corporations as the basis for exchange, Fleischacker notes, "His real point is precisely the opposite: that advanced economies are marked by a plethora of small, independent trades that fit into one another without deliberate organization" (Fleischacker, 2004, 11). If this is Smith's vision, I think I could affirm it. I have no romantic illusions about national-socialist institutions running an economics through impersonal, bureaucratic forces. Only utopian ideologues deny how badly that project turned out. However, if this is Smith's vision, as Fleischacker suggests, then the question it raises is why did it not work? Where is Smith's market? This does not seem to be the "market" the Smithian tradition has produced anymore than the contemporary mainline Protestant or Catholic Church is the church Augustine or Aquinas (let alone Jesus) envisioned.

Perhaps the tradition got hijacked? Or perhaps it had within it a contrary sentiment that led to the agonistic view of exchange that I witnessed at that shrimp and lobster plant? I do think that such an agonistic dogma is also part of Smith's commonsense tradition, and the unquestioned assumption of this dogma has led to a heretical dogmatism (heretical to the Christian faith) that can finally not sustain such a vision of the world. In this sense, I find it interesting that the Mennonite Community, known as "Reba Place," has been more successful in embodying the "orthodox" Smithian vision than the Smithian tradition itself. How do we account for this?

Is it possible that something like the Christian vision at Reba Place makes possible a more fruitful conservation of the orthodox Smithian tradition than the current global market and its exaltation of freedom? This would be a wonderful irony. The antagonistic individual freedom of the current market place, and the corporations that look only to maximize profits, pits poor working women in Honduras against individual fast-food consumers in North America and produces large, impersonal multinational forms of exchange that are incapable of being ordered to natural or Christian virtues. Those forms of exchange would claim Adam Smith as their father. But a small Christian community that would never claim Smith among the communion of saints has been able to preserve something like his vision much more than Red Lobster, Wal-Mart, or Nike. Why is that? Could it have something to do with God or the 'god' each tradition set forth?

GOD AND ADAM SMITH

Adam Smith never avowed atheism, but he certainly expressed heretical views, and did so without concern for consequences once he no longer held a chair in Moral Philosophy at the University of Glasgow (Fleischacker, 2004, 15). Smith, like Shaftesbury, treated god as an item of common sense. They were both religious pluralists who tolerated any doctrine of god as long as it passed a moral test in that it contributed to human sociality. Smith's philosophy eschewed metaphysics and, by implication, any significant engagement with theological doctrine. Instead, he looked to the everyday. For this reason, Fleischacker sees Smith as an "anticipation of Wittgenstein" who does to economics what the latter did to language; they both show us the reasonableness of the everyday and, thus, they are both suspicious of philosophy. But there is a crucial difference Fleischacker overlooks; Wittgenstein thought we were held captive to philosophy because of our ordinary language, because of how the exchanges mislead us into thinking such things as that our language is private. We needed a therapy to overcome this captivity. Smith valorizes the ordinary in a way that never raises this question about economic exchanges. Everyday signs are natural; they are what they are.

Smith offers a theological defense of these natural signs, leading to a correlational theology that finally makes theology superfluous. Fleischacker recognizes the problems inherent in this position. They lose the ability to be self-critical. He states, "An important objection to any sort of common-sense philosophy is that it may leave us with no room for criticizing our ordinary views, that it can collapse into uncritical faith in whatever dogmas happened to be abroad in society" (Fleischacker, 2004, 25). What might that dogma be? Here is where I think Fleischacker and Smith are both right and wrong. Of course, every form of ordinary exchange assumes dogma and this is inescapable because exchanges take place in terms of signs and dogma is nothing but authorized signs, things we believe or take on credit. The temptation with dogma is not that we have it; it is always with us and most dangerous when we think we freed ourselves from it. The temptation with dogma is that it becomes uncritical. Then it becomes dogmatism. We do not avoid dogmatism by falsely thinking we can avoid dogma, for that would require a form of life without exchange at all. The question then is which dogmas and how can we have a proper critical appreciation of them?

Smith was the inheritor of a natural theology which assumed a Stoic doctrine of providence, which, to me, is the consistency between *The Moral Sentiments* and *The Wealth of Nations* (Long, 2000, 75). Once again, I think I am restating, not questioning, Fleischacker's interpretation of Smith. He explains Smith's invocation of a "providential God" by acknowledging, "In each of these passages, however, the invocation of God goes along with an entirely naturalistic, secular account of how the phenomenon in question works." Thus, Smith does not simply say that God gave us notions of justice so that society would survive; he also shows how systems of justice arouse from our natural feelings of resentment, and are enforced in part because we realize that the fabric of society would disintegrate otherwise. . . . As far as I can see, the mention of God or Providence is not necessary to the argument of any empirical claim in TMS, much less to any claim in WN, which does not even make use of religious and teleological language" (Fleischacker, 2004, 45).

As a theologian who cares about how we speak about God, I want to say "Right, and that is the problem." For Smith, everything that theology does can be done by something else; it can be done by nature. This is the dogma by which he makes reference to God so all his references are basically harmless, unless you actually think God matters. What role is left for God then? Fleischacker notes that Smith "consistently gives religion an important role in morality" for God is the "great benevolent and all-wise Being, who directs all the movements of nature" (Fleischacker, 2004, 70–71). Much like Kant, Smith's religion is a "pure and rational religion" that anticipates a "universal moral religion" (Fleischacker, 2004, 71–72).

Adam Smith produces a tradition of a global market that can speak about God without it making the slightest bit of difference. The practices of exchange that have been generated from the Smithian tradition continue to speak about god, whether the name is used explicitly or incognito as human desiring, willing, preferring, nature, or just the way things are. For example, Baumol and Blinder in their *Economics, Principles and Policy* discuss the irrational nature of rent controls for the poor by making a dogmatic theological appeal to Smith's invisible hand, which they never own as a form of dogmatism. They explain the inevitable negative unintended consequences of rent controls as "battling the invisible hand" which is a peculiarity found in "lawmakers and rulers . . . from Rome to Pennsylvania" (Baumol and Blinder, 1991, 102). Note that both the church and the state have to bow before the dogma that intending to do good by providing rent controls to the poor produces more harm than simply allowing the signs of the current market exchange do their work.

Yet, Reba Place Fellowship is a counterfactual argument to this so-called natural or providential invisible hand. Because they share a common life, in doctrine, sacrament, and practice, they have been able to provide rent to poorer families well below market rates and still maintain the viability of their enterprise, which leads me to believe that the Smithian tradition speaks about God falsely. What it neglects is that the signs by which we exchange with each other are never *only* natural; they are always also produced. We make them, even as we also participate in God's economy. Because we do not want to ask what it would take to make signs like those made at Reba Place, we appeal to dogmas and tell each other that they cannot be other. Once we read exchanges at the lobster plant, at the drive-up window at McDonald's, at Wal-Mart, and so forth, in terms of the exchanges which occur in our common life at church, those Smithian dogmas cannot, for long, be uncritically accepted.

# Part II

## THE CORPORATION AND EVERYDAY ECONOMIC LIFE
### A Traditioned Theological Inquiry

# CORPORATIONS AND THE ENDS WE SERVE

The corporation is a creature of law—a legal artifice. Nobody has ever seen one. (Palmiter, 2003, 3)

How should Christians think about the corporation? This is not a question simply for CEOs, bishops, theologians, or business majors. It is a pressing question for every Christian because corporations make possible our daily food, our electricity, our transportation, our shelter, our clothing, and everything else that sustains daily existence. This must be recognized, because if we neglect it we simply live by denial of the conditions that make our lives possible. What gives us daily life cannot be radically evil. The Christian faith does have a healthy suspicion against many business practices, but that rightful suspicion should not turn into jeremiad protest or benign neglect. If it does the former, theologians simply appear foolish.

We all work for, and exist within, corporations. We depend upon them. To then turn and offer a jeremiad against them without, of course, withdrawing from them, is obviously to fail to account for our everyday life. How can we, in practice, affirm them and, in theory, deny them? Neither will it do to treat them with a benign neglect, as if they are not matters for theological analysis. They are creatures, even if quite odd ones, and thus we must think through their theological significance. We should do this, as we did in the first part of this work, by thinking about first principles and ends.

While Christian faith assumes one supernatural end for all of creation—to know, love, and enjoy God forever—it also recognizes various natural ends that can, and should, be ordered toward that supernatural end. As long as these natural ends recognize that they are also means, they have a proper role in God's economy. When they become ends in themselves and are not open to ends beyond themselves, to goodness, truth, beauty, and ultimately God, then they become vicious. The Christian virtues and vices are means to help us assess when this occurs, for it is not always easy to recognize. All corporations are not the same. Some are faithful; some are faithless. This chapter examines the ends corporations serve and points in the direction of the virtues and vices such ends assume. The next sets a context for understanding the virtues and vices monetary exchange can serve.

What is "the corporation" and how does it fit within God's economy for the flourishing of human persons? I will address this question from a perspective of the ends "persons" serve and the virtues and vices such ends produce. However, this is no easy task because of the complexity of the question. This question contains many theological assumptions, which lead to further more complicated questions. Take the basic question of whether we should expect the corporation to promote or prohibit the cultivation of those virtues that orient a person to her or his proper end? Such an expectation will itself be contested. But this contested question assumes some basic theological knowledge as to what constitutes a person's proper end, which will also be contested. If we expect the corporation to orient us to a proper end, which end is it? Would it be a natural or a supernatural end, and what is the relationship between them? Does the human person have a "double finality" where a natural end exists—separate from a supernatural end—or does the human person have a natural orientation to a supernatural end so that only one end (the supernatural end) gives him his true meaning?

If we expect corporations to produce virtues, then what constitutes the human creature's proper end will determine which virtues we think corporations should produce. If we have a natural end distinct from any supernatural one, then we should expect an orientation toward moral virtues such as justice, temperance, prudence, and courage. If these two ends are not finally distinct, then we would expect a good and faithful corporation to contribute directly or indirectly to the theological virtues of faith, hope, and charity as well.

However, the expectation that the corporation orients us to either a moral or theological end will be immediately challenged by some, especially by those in the Christian liberal tradition (or the neoconservatives) who make clear demarcations among political, cultural, and economic spheres. They see the corporation as a neutral mechanism that depends upon moral and cultural values it cannot produce itself, for the corporation is primarily "an investment vehicle for the pooling of money and labor" (Palmiter, 2003, 3).

I would not ask my automobile to order me to a natural or supernatural end. Why would I expect a "vehicle" like the corporation to be any different? Asking whether the corporation promotes the common good and contributes to human flourishing would be akin to asking whether the automobile does so. It is not the corporation that does this, but the cultural sphere within which the corporation as a neutral vehicle travels. The corporation may have some indirect relation to the common good and human flourishing, but it should not be expected to address concerns for which it was not created. The corporation is a neutral vehicle that neither produces virtue or vice; it merely reflects the cultural values that sustain it.

I do not find this position reasonable for it posits distinct cultural, political, and economic spheres and overlooks how these spheres are always already mixed. The corporation is made possible and sustained by a rigid and highly regulated political and legal system; it is a legal artifice. Moreover, it produces culture, as much as it is produced by it. However, that is only to assert a position that still needs argumentation. Any adequate argument will need to address at least these two sets of questions:

1. For what end does the corporation (a legal person) exist, and how does that end relate to the end for which human persons exists?
2. If we expect the corporation to orient us to an end, should we consider that end natural, and therefore primarily related to moral virtues such as justice, temperance, prudence, and courage? Or should we expect it to orient us to a supernatural end as well, and therefore to theological virtues such as faith, hope, and charity?

There are four possible responses to the second question. First, we may expect corporations *explicitly* to assist Christians and all reasonable people in those virtues that orient us to our natural or supernatural ends, to the moral or theological virtues. Second, we might expect them to do this, but to do it *implicitly* rather than explicitly. Third, our expectations might be somewhat more modest. We expect corporations, at most, to do no harm—which is to say, we should expect them not to cultivate in us those vices and sins that disorder our lives and keep us from attaining the moral and theological virtues that lead to human flourishing. Finally, perhaps we should have no expectation that the corporation orders us to either a natural or supernatural moral end. It is a neutral mechanism that depends upon cultural or political values it cannot and does not produce.

These two sets of questions and four possible responses form the basis for this chapter. I will return to these four responses after examining more fully the two questions, for we will be able to see more clearly the significance of these four possible responses only after examining more fully the questions.

### THE ENDS OF LEGAL PERSONS (CORPORATIONS) AND HUMAN PERSONS

What is the end of the corporation and how does it relate to the end of human flourishing? This is not an easy question to answer, but I think it important to recognize that definitions alone will not settle any disputes. Simply stating that freedom defines the flourishing of the human person or maximization of profits defines the corporation, even though both are true, accomplishes very little. This is to work with a faulty use of language where we assume the meaning of words is found in ostensive definitions. This neglects the important philosophical advance of "meaning holism" over "logical positivism." The latter assumed that the meaning of a word is found when we carefully define our terms and then use them consistently such that they either point to something specific (positivism) or always bear a logical tautology. The efforts to give language this kind of precision failed and always will fail. Few reasonable philosophers still hold to the logical positivist hope of a precisely specified meaning through definition. As Wittgenstein taught us, language cannot be scientific in that sense. Instead, meaning is use. By that, he did not mean that language means whatever I want it to mean, but that meaning is not primarily nor exclusively found through ostensive definitions. Meaning emerges through the uses to which language is put.

Catholic philosophers, like Alasdair MacIntyre and Charles Taylor, have been pressing this point for some time. MacIntyre calls this "narrative intelligibility." Taylor draws on the philosophical tradition of meaning holism, but the principle is the same. Meaning is not secured by a definition, but its use.

This is important because the Catholic liberal tradition tends to argue through a kind of logical positivism. They offer a basic definition of the human person in terms of freedom and then equate that definition with the "freedom" that neoliberal economics extols. Therefore, Catholic liberalism always finds a congruence between John Paul II's account of freedom in *Centesimus Annus* and freedom in the liberal, capitalist tradition. Nevertheless, if we recognize that meaning is use, then we get a richer account of language that allows for what Taylor calls "strong evaluation." We will have to place the term *freedom* in a richer narrative context rather than just compare weak definitions in order to determine the compatibility or incompatibility between Christian freedom and liberal freedom.

Let me give what I take to be two telling examples. Doug Bandow and William McGurn both find the modern corporation set within the context of the free market consistent with the Christian anthropology set forth by John Paul II in *Centesimus Annus*. Both McGurn and Bandow stand in, what McGurn calls, "the Christian liberal tradition," which is not to be confused with the "liberal Christian tradition" (Blank and McGurn, 2004, 140). This tradition assumes that the freedom necessary for capitalist exchange is consistent with the freedom that grounds John Paul II's anthropology. As McGurn puts it, "The pope tells us that man's destiny is freedom" (Blank and McGurn, 2004, 88). Because free markets allow human beings to use their "spiritual" freedom to create wealth, their exchanges are congruent with this Christian anthropology. Bandow also embraces the freedom set forth in a liberal economic order. He writes, "Christians, and the Christian church, can use the broad freedom afforded by a liberal society to encourage the members of that society to embrace the richer, saving freedom of faith" (Bandow and Schindler, 2002, 340).

Or as Richard Neuhaus, another proponent of the Christian liberal tradition puts it, "*Centesimus Annus* is about the free society, including economic freedom." The logical argument in this tradition seems to go like this: John Paul II gives us the definition of a

Christian anthropology as freedom. The *free* market also assumes persons should be free to enter into exchanges. It may not always achieve this end; and sometimes sinful people, as they are wont to do, misuse this freedom for improper ends, but the best congruence between a Christian anthropology defined by freedom and an economic system is, by definition, a free market.

Finding fault with the logic of this position is difficult, except for the very kind of logic that it employs. It assumes the kind of logical positivism noted above. It uses the term *freedom* as an ostensive definition that correlates a thing in the human person with a lack of regulation in economic exchange and equates them. If instead of this kind of logic, we invoke meaning holism a rather different account of freedom emerges. The term "freedom" cannot be given its meaning simply by a definition that designates a discrete thing, but how it gets used. When we examine how freedom gets used in the Christian liberal tradition, its meaning takes on a more complex and problematic hue than simple appeals to definitions allow.

Note how McGurn's use of freedom leads to positions difficult to square with Catholic social teaching. For instance, he questions the role of government to legislate against child labor based on the real possibilities afforded an Asian child who works in a garment factory sewing clothes for Wal-Mart. He, by no means, defends child labor, but he wants to make his "American" audience aware of the market realities this child faces. He writes, "An Asian audience would immediately recognize that the real alternative for that Bangladesh girl would not be trundling off to class but scavenging through garbage heaps or prostituting herself." And he concludes: "To our sensibilities, this is not an attractive trade-off. But in real life poor people typically do not have the choices we wish them to have, and the market sometimes brings better choices even when that is not its intention. While it might soothe Western consciences to eliminate child labor through regulations, in reality we may—if successful—be forcing children into something worse" (Blank and McGurn, 2004, 132). In other words, the unintended consequences of government regulations against child labor will be worse than the unregulated free market realities that give an Asian child a choice between prostitution and child labor. In legislating against child labor, we unintentionally send a child into prostitution. The conclusion seems to be that we should not regulate against such practices, but let the unregulated free market provide options for children who do not have them.

If we think of freedom in terms of simple definitions, then we see that an option for child labor, instead of prostitution, does not stand in any serious contradiction to the freedom McGurn finds consistent with John Paul II's teaching. But how can this be? McGurn's argument could also be used to explain the real life situation people confront when it comes to abortion, but why does he not raise that as well? How does this form of argument square with the following quote from *Veritatis Splendor*, where John Paul draws on *Gaudium et Spes* to set forth "intrinsic evils"?

> Reason attests that there are objects of the human act which are, by their nature, "incapable of being ordered" to God, because they radically contradict the good of the person made in his image. These are the acts which, in the Church's moral tradition, have been termed 'intrinsically evil (*intrinsece malum*): they are such *always* and *per se*, in other words, on account of their very object, and quite apart from the ulterior intentions of the one acting and the circumstances. . . . The Second Vatican Council itself, in discussing the respect due to the human person gives a number of examples of such acts: "Whatever is hostile to life itself, such as any kind of homicide, genocide, abortion, euthanasia and voluntary suicide; whatever violates the integrity of the human person, such as mutilation, physical and mental torture and attempts to coerce the spirit; whatever is offensive to human dignity, such as subhuman living conditions, arbitrary imprisonment, deportation, slavery, prostitution and trafficking in women and children, degrading conditions of work which treat labourers as mere

instruments of profit and not as free responsible persons. . . ." (para. 80; Wilkins, 1999, 150)

Note how different the use of freedom is in *Veritatis Splendor* and *Gaudium et Spes* in comparison to its use in the Christian liberal tradition with its consequential logic. Can we really find a moral distinction between child labor and prostitution, both of which are intrinsic evils, such that we can prefer an unregulated market because it at least allows a child the freedom to choose between them? This raises the question whether the Christian liberal tradition can avoid utilitarian arguments.

Take a second example. I have tried to find a case study I thought those of us in the anti-liberal Christian tradition could make common cause with those in the Christian liberal tradition. It is an example of a shrimp and lobster factory that was part of a global fast-food corporation. It took the food from the waters off the coast of Honduras, prepared them with Honduran labor, paying them wages such that they could not afford to buy the very food that they produced—whereas it could be shipped to landlocked people to be consumed at fast-food restaurants as entertainment. I assumed, based on the teaching in *Veritatis Splendor* quoted above, that this was an example of an intrinsically evil action. I wrote, "the very men and women that risked securing and processing this food, the men and women whose hands were the conditions for making lobster and shrimp available as consumable food items for others, were then excluded from consuming the produce they made available. This was (and is) clearly an unjust situation. No theologian (I hope) would intentionally defend these kinds of exploitative practices" (Bandow and Schindler, 2003, 82).

I was surprised then, when Bandow disagreed that this was an intrinsically unjust situation. He suggested "that situation could have resulted from entrepreneurial insight and the honest investment of money fairly earned, resulting in the creation of a company that pays market wages as promised and benefits that may well exceed any comparable ones in the community, region, or even nation" (Bandow and Novak, 2003, 333). When, in Catholic social teaching, did market wages alone demonstrate the justice of economic exchange? When the Christian liberal tradition defines freedom, we must remember that these kinds of practices determine the context that gives that term its intelligibility.

Simple definitions of terms such as *freedom, the corporation, capitalism,* and *the free market* are abstractions that have limited usefulness. No such singular entities exist; they are platonic ideals (in the bad sense philosophers often critique). The corporation is an idealized essence that has no existence outside the virtual legal space in which it is produced. Thus, we cannot define the corporation as if we are speaking of a single entity and ask how it fits within God's good economy. We must speak about particular corporations and note their significance by the larger narratives that give them their meaning. For example, the Maytag corporation, which for the sake of truth and integrity honored a faulty advertisement for free airfare with every purchase, should not be granted the same status as Arthur Andersen, which used its ethics department to bilk its clients (see Toffler, 2003). Corporations, like people, may share an essence, but they exist in different shapes and sizes, especially when acting morally.

The corporation does have a basic definition and purpose, which is established by law. It is a fictive legal person that exists to maximize profit. This does make the fictive legal person of the corporation somewhat different from that of the human person in the liberal tradition; for by its insistence on the priority of the right over the good the latter eschews particular ends for the acting person. Each person must be an individual who chooses his or her own end. The case of the "person" of the corporation is a bit more complex. On the one hand, it too must be an individual that supposedly chooses its own end outside of political or theological regulations. On the other hand, the fictive individual of the corporation has a set end legally enforceable. As previously noted, the basic definition of a corporation is "an investment vehicle for the pooling of money and labor" whose purpose is singular—to maximize profits (Palmiter, 2003, 3). This should be an uncontested definition of the corporation's end, but it does not yet settle any controversy among Christians who find the modern liberal business corporation antithetical or amenable to a Christian anthropology.

That corporations exist to maximize profits is not, in itself, offensive to Christian teaching if that maximization of profits does not conflict with the virtues. Both Maytag and Arthur Andersen sought to maximize profits. One thought this was best achieved through virtuous means, the other through vicious ones. Both made decisions primarily based on economic consequences. Maytag was not honoring the one practical consequence of Kant's categorical imperative when they honorably chose to never tell a lie; their decision was based on maintaining the trust of the consumer and living consistent with the faith tradition of its owner. Arthur Andersen's inability to tell the truth did have negative consequences for its corporate viability. However, and this is the key, neither corporation's actions can be assessed on moral grounds other than profit maximization. This is the end corporations serve. It is the reason investors enter into exchanges with them. Like the modern individual, it has rights without duties for it has no direct relationship to a common good except profit maximization. This is a descriptive claim given the legal context within which corporations operate. And here is the central problem in any discussion of the corporation and the human person. The corporation has the legal status of a fictive individual, along with many of the rights individuals possess in modern political society. However, the corporation is not assumed to have the same moral obligations persons do, especially as those obligations are defined by the church.

This greatly distances the modern corporation from the Medieval *societas*, which was assumed to have a different kind of moral agency than the liberal individual, which the modern corporation is. The modern corporation is a legal construct based on the ideal situation of the autonomous individual whose freedom is secured through right. The societas was assumed to work within the context of the virtues; it is why Aquinas discussed it within that context. The modern corporation is never discussed within the context of the virtues; it is discussed solely in terms of law.

Corporations have two basic kinds of relationships. They have internal relations based on a rather fixed and standard structure and external relations to all the constituencies that make them possible, but do not directly operate its internal affairs. As Robert Palmiter explains it, "'outside' relationships with creditors, suppliers, customers, employees, and government authorities usually are subject to legal norms that treat the corporation as a person—such as laws of contract, debtor-creditor, antitrust, labor and tax" (Palmiter, 2003, 5). The assumption that the corporation is "free" to pursue interests outside of legal regulation is one of the great misnomers set forth by contemporary critics of the "free" market. As "persons," corporations in the late modern era are as overregulated and regimented as any other individual. Corporations do not embody a hedonistic and permissive form of liberty that amounts to a freedom from specific ends; to assume otherwise places the problem with late-modern corporations at the wrong place.

As Slavoj Zizek argues, this is a worn-out cliché about late modernity that avoids the obvious: "It is today's apparently hedonistic and permissive postmodern reflexive society which is paradoxically more and more saturated by rules and regulations that allegedly promote our well-being" (Zizek, 2000, 132). This is as true with the corporation as fictive individual as it is with other individuals.

The theological reservation we must have with the modern corporation is not that it is unregulated, but that it is regulated to pursue only its single end of profit maximization. Lawrence Mitchell names well this "fundamental flaw." The modern corporation depends on, and perpetuates, an eighteenth-century liberal ideal of autonomy, individualism, and unencumbered choice. The corporation is treated in law and culture as an individual whose main *moral* obligation is to maximize profit for stockholders in the short term. But as a fictive individual, it bears no moral responsibility for its protected rights (Mitchell, 2001, 54–56).

If we assume that the difficulty with corporations is their freedom from specific *teloi*, then we might be tempted to suggest that the solution to this difficulty is more and stronger regulation. However, this overlooks one crucial question—to what end? It could be that a central difficulty with the modern corporation is not its freedom from ends, but that it embodies the illusion of the modern individual, which is to say that by falsely assuming it has overcome a teleological ordering, it has forgotten the end it serves and, thus, fails to present that end for public accountability.

### CREATED NATURE AND SUPERNATURAL ORIENTATIONS

Corporations are fictive individuals enacted, by law through state legal systems, for the specific purpose of maximizing profit by pooling resources. This does not tell us much; it only sets the context within which we must discern significant differences among corporations. Does this permit or prohibit created nature to achieve its end? An answer to that question depends on what we assume the end of created nature to be. If we adopt the position of a single end to human creatures based on a natural vision for God, then the corporation—as a natural institution—will need to be understood and assessed in terms of the supernatural order. It does not inhabit some neutral, secular space where such assessment would be improper and only applicable to the culture in which the corporation as a neutral mechanism functions.

This would not deny a proper independence for corporations from the church, but it would assume that they bear some responsibility to the church's teachings. The very fact that a rich tradition of Catholic social teaching from *Rerum Novarum* to *Centesimus Annus* boldly speaks to all the participants in market exchanges as if they should listen, suggests that a rigid double finality cannot make sense of the Spirit's leading of the church's teaching. The church has something to teach everyone engaged in everyday economic exchanges. The tacit anthropological background that renders these teachings intelligible would look something like de Lubac's reading of Aquinas where that institution entrusted with Divine teaching, the church, illumines, perfects, and corrects natural reason. The human creature has a single vocation, which would be a supernatural orientation. The church's tradition of speaking to the corporate world assumes a role for our supernatural orientation. This does not turn the corporation into the church, but suggests that it cannot be understood and assessed solely on natural ends. No secular space independent from God's purposes exists.

If we adopt a neoscholastic doctrine of a double finality, where the human creature has both a natural and a supernatural end, then theologians' expectations for the corporation will fundamentally differ from those which assume a single end. More independence will be conceded to certain natural institutions that could then be understood through reason alone. Of course, this still raises the question "which reason?" Which account of economic reasoning should we concede as natural? Neoliberalism with its "marginalist" rationality and call for free markets as is found in the Christian liberal tradition? Keynesianism with its insistence on government intervention? Marxism with its call for a revolutionary form of exchange as found among liberation theologians? Are Adam Smith's three principles of competitive markets the basis for a natural economic rationality: act only on self-interest, provide full information to all participants, and let them participate without any coercion? Or should we think more in terms of Keynes's multiplier effect which assumes government must step in and provide injections of capital from outside the free operation of markets? Or should we adopt Ricardo-Marx's labor theory of value? And, of course, many other positions on economic rationality exist, but no universally accepted form yet prevails. Theologians can be found who claim each of these positions is the one reason best established. Can any of them claim that their position is the natural economic rationality?

If we accept the neoscholastic principle of a double finality, it still does not settle the issue as to what would constitute a natural understanding of the role of the corporation based on reason alone. It will still need to be argued for, but for what would it be arguing? Is there a singular, natural, economic rationality waiting to be discovered? The mere presence of a multitude of natural, economic rationalities by no means denies the possibility of a "metaphysically realist" position whereby we might some day discover the true and uncontested natural economic reason, but I think we would be hard pressed to argue we possess it today. Nor do I think most reasonable persons would think such a form of rationality exists—given the kind of practical reason economics, as a science, must be.

How we understand the common good and human flourishing will differ (perhaps not decisively) based on our response to these two influential theological positions: first, that the human creature has a singular supernatural end characterized by a natural desire for the vision of God; and second, that the human creature has a two-fold end, one natural and fully knowable by reason alone, the other supernatural and known only by faith. Both these positions are versions of the important Thomistic theme "grace perfects nature," but the force of the "perfects" differs between them. In the first, *perfects* suggests "illumines" as well as "completes." That is to say, nature is not a self-evident category to which grace is an addition; what constitutes our "nature" remains somewhat mysterious to us such that Jesus reveals not only what it means to be God, but also creature. Thus, what we expect reason alone to accomplish will have greater limitations on it than if we adopt the second position. It assumes that we know nature without any divine supplement, for if we did not know it how could we know that God has visited and assumed our nature?

The first position can be seen in John Milbank's insistence that the natural needs to be "supernaturalized." It leads to dissatisfaction with the modern corporation, arguing that it must be "socialized from within" in order for it to be oriented toward the one, true end of all creation—which is friendship with God. The second position can be seen in Romanus Cessario's insistence that we must have a metaphysically realist understanding of created nature, reliably knowable by reason alone if we are to understand the divine mystery. Thus, he states, "the very doctrine of the incarnation implies a twofold order of being, truth, and knowledge: that of created nature (assumed by the Word) and that of the uncreated God and his grace."

What is the relationship between created nature and supernature reason and faith? Cessario states, "the order of nature is distinct from and has no claim upon the supernatural (Griffiths and Hütter, 2005, 332, 336). This is unobjectionable. Created nature has no "claims" on God. Grace is not owed creatures. Consider though, what claim does the supernatural have on the natural? In other words, is "nature" transparent to reason alone? Or does it best come into view through the hypostatic union, that unity of divine and human that can only be seen in the Person of Jesus? The deeper question Henri de Lubac addressed is if nature has its own end independent from supernature that can be known outside of the gift of grace?

How different are the two positions represented by Milbank and Cessario? If we assume the *duplex ordo* as distinct orders, then this will underwrite the claim that the ends the corporation serves are consistent with reason alone. We would not expect it to attend to Holy Scripture or the teaching of Christian tradition. Although the latter provides important considerations for the culture within which corporations function, those primarily working within corporations should not be bound by them. They should listen more to economists than theologians. McGurn would have lower expectations for the role of the corporation; it should function within a natural moral reason that can be known apart from faith. We have fairly reliable information as to what this natural moral reason is and, thus, based on this reliable information, we know that the modern corporation, while never a salvific institution, can easily be made consistent with Christian teaching.

If we assume the human person is defined by her or his supernatural end, then we will have higher expectations for the role of corporations within the divine economy. They are not understood as neutral vehicles, but theologically significant. Thus, they must at least do no harm and, at best, they should be ordered by a theological rationality—implicit or explicit. This should not lead to the conclusion that economic or business rationality must always explicitly serve the ends of faith. No one should expect members of a corporation to begin their day by citing the Nicene Creed—this is not the point. Anyone who makes such a claim would be hard pressed to live it consistently in everyday life. I doubt Christians inspect the confessional stances of those with whom they engage in trade anymore than they desire the airline pilot has a proper Christology when they board an airplane. The point is not to turn the corporation into a confessional institution; it is to recognize that, for the baptized, their work in the corporation must be able to be offered to God's glory. No neutral secular space exists outside the vocation to offer our labor as such a gift. At the minimum, this requires that we not let our labor produce vices in us or others. At a maximum, we should not be surprised if opportunities arise to receive gifts of faith, hope, and charity through our daily labor.

We should think of the relationship between the corporation and natural or supernatural ends, much as we think of the relationship between faith and reason. Reinhard Hütter and Paul Griffiths offer a temperate account of this relation when they remind us that some things are knowable by faith, some by reason, and some by both.

They offer three important conclusions with regard to this relationship that can help illumine how Christians should think about the corporation. First, "faith will never become the only kind of reasoning that Christians use or need." Theologians must not think they bear the burden of constructing alone through divine teaching a global economic system. Other kinds of reasoning will always be necessary in everyday business exchange. This may be something as simple as a more efficient way to hang sheetrock by an individual contractor or thinking through the significance of the devaluation of the Chinese Yuan on interest rates in the U.S. housing market. Second, "deliverances of faith have, for Christians, certitude; they are irrefragably correct." Those places where we have clear teachings on economic matters in Scripture and tradition are not to be ignored. We cannot ignore the clear teaching in Acts 2 and 4 that we are to hold our property not as individuals but "in communion." Moreover, consequentialist reasoning cannot order something properly which is intrinsically disordered. Third, "once the disposition for faith becomes active, it transfigures and reframes every form of reasoning" (Griffiths and Hütter, 2005, 10, 12). Although Christians should not expect explicit divine teachings on the most efficient way to hang sheetrock or consider currency devaluation, faith cannot be absent even from such natural forms of reasoning.

Directly or indirectly, faith as a form of reasoning matters in everyday life. No one should mark out a neutral territory and suggest it is off limits to faith, solely the province of the social scientists, even if we cannot always see its relevance. We must seek to discern the relevance of faith in all things.

I am not arguing that every economist, business executive, worker, or consumer must explicitly confess Christ for his or her work to fit within God's economy. Theologians no more assume such a reality than do others who buy products at reasonable prices. Our everyday exchanges do not require explicit confessions of Christian faith, nor should they. Nevertheless, if we confess that all things are created in, through, and for Christ, then the significance of Christology or Trinity for economic reflections should be appropriate. Simply because theologians assess economic exchanges based on the richness of Christian doctrine does not entail that we are then seeking to generate an entire economics from Christian confessions. We must try to show, however, what difference the fullness of Christian teaching makes for our economic exchanges.

Earlier I noted four possible theological responses to the question how the end the corporation serves fits with the end the human person serves. I argued that the modern corporation is a virtual individual bounded by law to have rights without moral obligations other than profit maximization. This has the sanction of U.S. law. In a classic court case, *Dodge v. Ford Motor Co.* (Mich. 1919) the Michigan Supreme Court found against Henry Ford's policy of slashing prices on his cars on the grounds that his company "has made too much money, has had too large profits . . . and sharing them with the public by reducing the price of the output of the company ought to be undertaken" (Palmiter, 2003, 188). Based on the claim held by stockholders that this threatened their profit maximization, the court ruled against Ford on the basis he operated as a "semi-eleemosynary institution and not as a business institution" (Palmiter, 2003, 188).[21]

This has been a foundational ruling that sets the ends corporations serve. Profit maximization, and never eleemosynary activities, set the context for any fiduciary duties corporate executives must pursue on the basis of the trust given to them by shareholders.

This, of course, is consistent with Adam Smith's famous quote from *The Wealth of Nations*: "It is not from the benevolence of the butcher, the brewer, or the baker, that we expect our dinner, but from their regard to their own interest. We address ourselves, not to their humanity but to their self-love, and never talk to them of our own necessities but of their advantages" (Smith, 1965, 14). The first part of this quote should be uncontroversial. I do hope that businesses that serve me in my community make a sufficient profit and those they employ make sufficient profit so they can remain in business and receive a solid, temperate living.

It is the second part of Smith's famous quote that should alarm people of faith. Should I not also expect these local businesses to address the necessities of our neighborhoods? If this is impermissible, then we are far from the sense of moral agency in which Aquinas set forth the *societas*.

For Aquinas, profit from a legitimate *societas* was not sinful, nor was the practice of economic exchange ever neutral. This is why he discussed it always within the context of the virtues and vices (*ST* II.II.78.2.rep. obj. 3; Aquinas, 1948). Economic exchanges are discussed within the context of sins against justice. Thus, the virtue of justice must be established first before we can speak well of the corporation's role in God's economy. Justice as a virtue is far from justice in procedural liberalism where, as Bandow suggested, what matters most is "honest investment of money fairly earned, resulting in the creation of a company that pays market wages as promised." That is a description of justice as proper procedure. However, justice as a virtue concerns a "habit whereby a man renders each one his due by a constant and perpetual will" which will render the one who exercises it "good" (*ST* II.II 58.1 and 3; Aquinas, 1948). This latter qualification suggests that justice assumes not only proper procedure but also an orientation toward the good. This cannot be accomplished if our only orientation is maximization of shareholder profit.

These kinds of concerns demonstrate, I hope, that the corporation cannot be considered as a neutral vehicle independent from moral and theological considerations. It is theologically significant. So should we then expect it to produce virtue explicitly or implicitly, or should we expect it to avoid vice? The answer is yes. I do think we should expect our daily labor to produce in us virtuous habits that orient us toward the good. Work consumes too much of our time to think that we only cultivate those habits in some separate cultural sphere and then bring them with us to the corporation. If the corporation is rightly ordered, it will be a place where we develop the habit of justice and since charity is finally the form of all the virtues, we should not expect it improper to speak of humanity's "necessities." At the least, we should not expect the corporation to produce vice in us.

The vice to which economic exchange tempts us is greed. Is the modern corporation exempt from this; does it tempt us more than the earlier forms of exchange? McGurn, like most of the Christian liberal tradition, has little time for the medieval tradition of economic analysis. He writes, "Today we chuckle over the scholastics of the Middle Ages, who never could overcome their problem with interest" (Blank and McGurn, 2004, 74). He also argues that modern markets do not produce the capital sin of greed. In fact, he accuses those who do not recognize the spirituality at the basis of capitalism of committing the capital sin of pride for refusing to see how these modern economic practices produce the virtue of solidarity (Blank and McGurn, 2004, 71–72). Is this adequate? Does the fiduciary duty of shareholder profit maximization orient us toward the capital vice of greed? If our minimum is to expect the corporation not to produce this vice in us, then we should more closely examine what this vice is. It is the reason scholastic theologians like Aquinas were concerned with interest and usury. They thought it served a false happiness.

What is interesting is that the very kind of false happiness Aquinas warns us of in *De malo* seems to be precisely what Christian liberal economic tradition advocates—desire growth without limit through mutual optimizing of utility. Can the modern corporation avoid this? We cannot answer yes or no; we must look to each particular corporation and recognize the variable degrees by which corporations do and do not fall prey to this temptation. The differences between Maytag and Arthur Andersen are prime examples of this. As long as corporations are generated within a legal context that assumes first that they are virtual individuals whose only fiduciary duty is shareholder profit maximization, then irrespective of the many good and virtuous people who work within them, the thrust of this all too modern individual will be towards greed. And it will reward those who pursue it. We will have to rethink the corporation within the terms of the Catholic Church rather than the global market in order to avoid having its only end as profit maximization. The last two chapters attempt to begin to do this. Before pursuing this, we must pause and assess whether the modern corporation can avoid the vice of pleonoxia, and we will need to examine this vice.

# — 6 —

## USURY

### Avarice as a Capital Vice

Has greed become good? Do we still have an understanding of deadly or capital vices, which should be avoided even if it would cause more, rather than less, suffering? What is greed and how does it relate to the virtues? It is usually discussed as a threat to the virtues of charity, justice, and liberality. It is also discussed in terms of the church's ancient usury prohibition, a scriptural injunction to lend without expecting a return. As we saw in the last chapter, this prohibition is now treated with quaint contempt, not only by economists, but also by moral theologians. Some good reasons may exist for this contempt, but usually it appears without any analysis of the usury prohibition. We must offer a strong evaluation of it in order to see why it mattered, and why it might still matter. I think that a concern to embody the virtues and avoid the vice of greed makes best sense of this ancient moral teaching.

Most economists would say that much of the church's teaching on economics had to be abandoned before human society could be advanced. This is particularly true of its prohibition of usury, a commandment Christianity shares with Judaism, Islam, and ancient "pagan" moralists. I will examine the peculiar history of the Christian church's teaching on usury in order to address the question whether this commandment—traditionally found in Exodus 22:23; Deuteronomy 23:19, 20; Leviticus 25:36, 37; Psalm 15:5; and Luke 6:36—advances social justice. But, of course, that term is often nothing more than a shibboleth. It makes little sense without a vision of what society should be. Laws like the usury prohibition and virtues such as justice and charity once gave us a vision of what society should look like.

The church's traditional teaching on usury has a complex history, but interpreting this history is not simply an exercise in nostalgia. Contemporary discussions on theology and metaphysics, on politics and economics, as well as ecumenical and interfaith relations would benefit from knowing the history of the usury prohibition for it bears on contemporary political, economic, ecumenical and interfaith relations. It might help us envision a good society. Differences and similarities among Christians, Jews, and Muslims, among Catholics, Protestants, and Anabaptists, among the many sects within Protestantism itself, and between people of faith and secularists result, in some degree, from the conflicted history surrounding usury. It also bears on economic class divisions and how we think about theology and metaphysics. Any good analysis of usury and money from the later Middle Ages into the early modern era must address the shift from realism to nominalism that characterized that transition. Given this important and complex history, the significance of usury's history has not been given its due in contemporary theological, political, and economic matters.

This is surprising for as much may have been written about the usury prohibition during the sixteenth century as was written about the doctrine "justification by faith alone." However, the lines of political demarcation are not easily disentangled. Protestants and Catholics were not all on one side, neither were Jews, Christians, and Muslims. People and movements opposed usury or supported exceptions to it for diverse reasons. Luther's opposition to usury was related to his opposition to Judaism, to the Catholic merchant Fugger family and their supporter, John Eck, and to his original support for the poor who suffered under usurious practices. But he found the Anabaptists going too far with their commitment to mutual aid. Anabaptists, many of whom were poor (or became poor), did not even question the usury prohibition (Klassen, 1964, 105.)[22] To lend at interest placed one under the ban. Their overriding concern was not some economic revolution; however, they were not proto-Marxists. Holiness motivated their teachings and actions.

Calvin, however, supported a qualified endorsement of money lent at interest for its own sake. He thought Catholicism bound conscience more tightly than Scripture warranted. His relaxation of the usury prohibition emerged from his sense of freedom.

Catholics also debated usury and its exception—especially Franciscans, Dominicans, and Jesuits. Division occurred even within these various orders. The distinction between usury and interest, various extrinsic titles that warranted interest payments, how the church's teachings were to be implemented—all these were subject to rigorous debate. Ironically, it has now been well argued that the Franciscan distinction between use and ownership, a distinction that contradicted Aquinas' consumptibility argument, did as much unintentionally to undercut the usury prohibition as anything. However, I would argue that all these debates and divisions are part of a common tradition. They fit within a debate about what it means to be a holy people. They are internal disagreements that could be resolved because they emerge from a common tradition of Christian practical wisdom.

However, with the Scottish Enlightenment, the church's tradition of moral reflection on the usury prohibition comes undone. An incommensurable conception of justice, charity, and practical reasoning emerges. Justice becomes fair procedure. Charity becomes private mutual benefit based on voluntary consent. And practical reasoning becomes calculative rationality. This tradition comes to

fruition in Jeremy Bentham's "Defence of Usury," when he wrote, "no man of ripe years, and of sound mind, ought out of lovingkindness to him, to be hindered from making such a bargain, in the way of obtaining money, as, acting with his eyes open, he deems conducive to his interest" (Bentham, 1952, 163). The difference between the secular rise of modern ethics after Bentham, and Christian reflection on economics prior to Bentham, involves a complete break in how one thinks about money. If "social justice" is defined in terms of this secular tradition, then the church's teaching can only be seen as reactionary, or as positively detrimental.

Secularism itself seems to be coming to an end—for good and ill. Some philosophers now speak of postsecular philosophy. Religion has returned as a powerful political and cultural movement, albeit often only ironically and sometimes in fundamentalist form. Moreover, Islamic culture, with its specific banking procedures that seek to avoid *riba* (usury), has garnered attention of both friend and foe of the secular free market system. Some find in it the possibility for a "third way" beyond socialism or capitalism (Buckley, 2000, 288, 299). The recovery of the Quranic teaching against usury has been part of the process of Islamicization. It is an intriguing development that seems to hold forth an alternative form of banking. As the International Association of Islamic Banks stated in what could easily be construed as a direct counter to Bentham and the liberal tradition, "Profitability—despite its importance and priority—is not therefore the sole criterion or the prime element in evaluating the performance of Islamic banks, since they have to match both between the material and the social objectives that would serve the interests of the community as a whole and help achieve their role in the sphere of social mutual guarantee" (Buckley, 2000, 308).

But this is not to say that the usury prohibition is an unambiguous good. For just as one finds in the Christian tradition of the usury prohibition a tacit anti-Judaism, so there is also such a potential for it in Quranic teaching. *Surah Al-Nisa* iv. 161 states, "We forbade the Jews good things which were formerly allowed them; because time after time they have debarred others from the path of God; because they practice usury—although they were forbidden it—and cheat others of their possessions" (Buckley, 2000, 187). Like similar claims in the Christian tradition, this easily leads to Jewish stereotypes and neglects the rich tradition of Jewish reflection on interest as well. In fact, Christians, Muslims, and Jews share a quest for holiness, albeit with significant differences in practice, which requires each of us to examine seriously the exchanges involved in lending and borrowing.

As already mentioned, Meir Tamari reminds us that the reason for the interest prohibition in the Torah is because of God's desire for a holy people produces the usury prohibition. This quest for holiness should also issue a serious caution about any direct merging of the modern nation state system with the ancient Christian, Jewish, or Islamic usury prohibition.[23] For I want to argue that the usury prohibition can only make sense in terms of a community of virtue, and this requires that it not be forced through state power. To enforce the usury prohibition through the legal, judicial, and political means of the nation state would be disastrous. As I shall argue later, it requires a community of virtue for it to make sense.

What bearing does the ancient Christian (as well as Islamic and Jewish) teaching have on modern economic life? This question has vexed theologians, economists, and bishops. Some read the history of the church's prohibition against usury as an irrational dogmatic commitment to Aristotelian and biblical principles that inevitably had to be abandoned once the Enlightenment's critical rationality subsumed scholastic economic principles (Böhm-Bawerk, Weber, Nelson). Others disagree with this reading, finding some continuity between modern and scholastic economics based on finding an "anticipatory approach" to modern economics latent in scholastic analysis, but what it anticipates differs (Langholm, 1992, 3). Some find in it the seeds for modern capitalism. Others find in it an anticipation of Marx's labor theory of value (Tawney). Still others see in it something more akin to Keynesianism (Keynes himself).

Still others find evidence in the usury prohibition for an economic "third way." Such was the Jesuit economist Bernard Dempsey who countered Keynes's effort to claim the scholastics for anticipating Keynesianism. Dempsey disagreed, but still claimed that the usury prohibition was valid in that it illumined problems with modern banking and credit institutions, which he characterized as "structural usury." Interestingly, both Catholic and evangelical Christian theologians are looking again to the usury prohibition as a way to think beyond the modern assumptions that our only economics options are global capitalism or socialism.

For all these very interesting historical studies of the usury prohibition, I think one crucial aspect is missing. They tend to examine usury solely from a legal perspective, but the usury prohibition is not best understood in terms of a modern ethics of obligation that focuses on law. It is easy to mistake the significance of the usury prohibition along these lines for it is, after all, a law-like proposition surrounded by an entire tradition of exceptions and extrinsic titles. Yet, perhaps we can understand the usury prohibition better now that even John Paul II, as well as a number of theologians and philosophers, have shown how the law primarily makes sense in terms of the virtues. This has primarily been done through the recovery of Aquinas and Aristotle for moral theology, something for which, of course, Christianity is in part indebted to Islam.

To simplify matters greatly, the complex history of the usury prohibition has the following main interpretations:

1. Modern economics as rejection of the church's dogmatic usury prohibition
2. The church's usury prohibition as anticipatory of:
   a. The rationality behind modern capitalism
   b. The labor theory of value
   c. Keynesianism

3. Scholastic economic analysis, along with the usury prohibition, as a "third way" beyond either capitalism or socialism

4. Virtue as that which renders intelligible the usury prohibition

Let me make brief comments on each of the above uses of the usury prohibition and then conclude by explaining how the virtue tradition helps make sense of it.

MODERN ECONOMICS AS REJECTION OF THE CHURCH'S DOGMATIC USURY PROHIBITION

Max Weber understood the history of usury as a necessary casuistic exercise in accommodating natural economic forces (Weber, 1978, 577). The usury prohibition reflected a primitive understanding of human community. The Deuteronomic legislation (Deut. 23:19-20) that allowed one to receive interest from foreigners but not from brothers is a sign of a small, primitive kinship group concerned primarily with personal exchanges, which allowed for charity. But this is undone once economics becomes rational. He stated:

> Rational economic association always brings about depersonalization and it is impossible to control a universe of instrumentally rational activities by charitable appeals to particular individuals. The functionalized world of capitalism certainly offers no support for any such charitable orientation. In it the claims of religious charity are vitiated not merely because of the refractoriness and weakness of particular individuals, as it happens everywhere, but because they lose their meaning altogether. Religious ethics is confronted by a world of depersonalized relationships which for fundamental reasons cannot submit to its primeval norms. (577)

For Weber, charity is primarily individual and personal. A rationalized economics is social and impersonal. The sectarian basis of the usury prohibition inevitably gave way to a more universal rationalized economics. This was inevitable because religious values cannot withstand "the world of facts"—"in the world of facts the inevitable compromises had to be made" (Weber, 1978, 585).

Weber's thesis is picked up by Benjamin Nelson who finds the inevitable compromises made in the history of the usury prohibition to be a transition from an economics based on "brotherhood" to one that becomes rationalized by "universal otherhood." Nelson follows Weber in finding the key transition to this rationalized modern ethic to be Calvinism and its rejection of the traditional prohibition of usury. Ernst Troeltsch tells a similar story. Calvin recognized the "productive power of money" and, thus, "rejected the canonical veto on usury and the scholastic theory of money, and on the contrary supported a doctrine of money, credit and usury which were nearer to the modern economic idea, with limitations . . ." (Troeltsch, 1981, 643).

The Weber thesis has tremendous popularity among economic historians. For instance, in his now classic *Worldly Philosophers* Robert Heilbronner distinguishes three types of response to the threat of economic disintegration. In so doing, he follows Weber closely albeit not identically. For Weber, economic action takes the form of "traditional," "value," or "calculative" rationality (Long, 2000, 67). Economic exchanges either fit within a tradition, are developed from some law-like deontological rule, or they become rationalized through individual choices in terms of marginal utility. Heilbronner's three economic types closely follow Weber's. There is first the "pull of tradition," second, the "whip of authority," and third, the modern "market system" where "society assured its own continuance by allowing each individual to do exactly as he saw fit." This he calls the "lure of gain" (Heilbronner, 1986, 18–21). Like Weber, he recognizes limitations in the third response, but once economic rationality is given these three alternatives, calculative rationality will always appear the most reasonable. Moreover, once these three types of economic rationality become our only alternative, the church's teachings will appear either to be nostalgic longing for tradition and organic community or deontological forms of theocratic oppression.

This narrative forms the social framework within which economists interpret economic history. It is the reason so many seem to read the history of modern economics as the overcoming of a moribund scholastic analysis. For instance, it is present in much of the Austrian school of economics.[24] Böhm-Bawerks monumental 1884 publication, *History and Critique of Interest Theories*, contained chapters such as "Resistance of economic practice to the canonistic prohibition of interest," "Victory in the Netherlands of school of economists who approved of interest," and "Backwardness of the romance countries: French legislators and writers cling tenaciously to the canonistic doctrine" (Böhm-Bawerk, 1959, 16–36). He began his historical assessment with the claim, "Since [the interest] controversy was at its height during the heyday of scholasticism, it can well be imagined that the growth in number of arguments and counter-arguments was by no means a measure of the growth in knowledge of the subject itself." Finding the medievals backward and their economics and business practices "a relapse in industry to the circumstances of primitive times," Böhm-Bawerk, much like Adam Smith before him, reaches back to pre-Christian Roman society for a more reasonable economics which tolerated interest. Thus historical progress begins in Roman society, gets thwarted in the Christian era until the rise of Protestantism and then returns with the modern era where the triumph of interest is the triumph of practical businessmen over abstract and theoretically minded ecclesiastics (Böhm-Bawerk, 1959, 9–17). This is the common secular narrative of the history of usury.

Those who see a complete rupture between the church's prohibition of usury and modern economics often view Calvin as the theologian who makes this rupture possible. Weber, Troeltsch, and Nelson share this social analysis. It privileges a peculiar reading of Calvinism where his overturning of the usury prohibition unintentionally lets loose the possibility of modern economics. This may be somewhat unfair to Calvin. After all, he did write, "To be certain, it would be desirable if usurers were chased from every country, even if the practice were unknown" (Boulton et al., 1994, 453). That is a far cry from Jeremy Bentham's "Defence of Usury." Was Calvin's teaching a radical shift in the tradition? Calvin did deny the sterility argument (money was barren), but so did many late scholastics. Calvin also recognized, as did the scholastics, that industry and not money alone produced profit. Moreover, he argued that since we could not ban usury altogether we should use it for the common good. Aquinas made a similar argument.[25] However, on one key point Calvin seems to differ from much of the scholastic tradition. He tended to understand justice primarily as increased utility where no one was harmed. So with respect to a mutually advantageous loan at interest, he asks, "Now what makes a contract just and honest or unjust and dishonest?" And he answers his question, "Has not the first fared better by means of an agreement involving usury by his neighbor than if the second had compelled him to mortgage or pawn his own goods?" (Boulton et al., 1994, 454).[26] Why does Calvin set forth mutual advantage as an argument for usury? Had this possibility been denied? Calvin seems to assume that mutual advantage alone makes the contract just.

This may be a key transition in economic rationality that begins to think of it solely in terms of marginal utility and abandons the understanding of charity and justice as virtues that place limits even on mutually beneficial exchanges. Is this the beginning of the modern conception of justice as primarily fair procedures and increased utility and charity as private and apolitical? Is Calvin to blame, or praise?

Many contemporary Christian ethicists find Calvin's ethics preferable assuming that he recognizes loans are not always exploitative of the poor because they can be mutually advantageous. Defenders of the usury prohibition are criticized for failing to understand how loans function, particularly the difference between loans for consumption and loans for production. Calvin is viewed as setting forth a new ethic free from the church's usury prohibition. But this is to misunderstand the church's teaching. It never argued that usury always oppressed the poor. Although it held that forth as a distinct possibility, it did not base the usury prohibition primarily, or even secondarily, on that possibility. Usury violated the virtuous communal possibilities of charity and justice, and this could occur even if the loan was mutually beneficial to all the persons involved. In losing the virtues of charity and justice, modern economics loses any significance of a teleological ordering of money. If money has no teleological limits, it becomes nothing but pure power. Jack Weatherford recognizes this inevitable trajectory in western conceptions of money. In his *History of Money,* he states, "The new money is raw power" (Weatherford, 1998, xii).

Calvinist evangelicals who seek to take seriously the biblical teaching against usury have a difficult time doing so, and finally sound like modern liberals because they often lack the resources to think of it in terms of the virtues that alone render it intelligible. Thus, David Jones argues in his *Reforming the Morality of Usury* that "the duty to love one's neighbor as oneself is most prominent and developed within John Calvin's thought." And this duty of love both permits and prohibits usury (Jones, 2004, 78–79, 136). What distinguishes permission from prohibition is whether the act allows one to love one's neighbor as one's self. However, once charity is understood as mutual advantage, then Christian ethics becomes as formalistic and empty as the Kantian categorical imperative.

### The Church's Usury Prohibition as Anticipatory of Modern Economics: Labor Theory of Value, Keynesianism, and Capitalism

John Noonan and Odd Langholm's analyses of usury offer a much improved and nuanced history than that of Weber, Troeltsch, Böhm-Bawerk, and Nelson. They show us how complex the story

of medieval economics is. Simple appeals to primitive kinship relations fail to explain the history of usury. Noonan offers a sober
historical analysis that seeks to avoid using the usury prohibition
for or against modern economics. He persuasively argues that the
church's usury prohibition is wrongly interpreted as primarily
dependent upon Aristotle and his understanding of money, for the
prohibition was in place long before Aristotle had been introduced
back into the West. He also shows how it is wrong to interpret the
usury prohibition as simply dependent upon the "economic conditions of the times." Moreover, he rejects the thesis that the scholastic analysis of usury was "related to the church's own interests."
The prohibition was defended even when it was not to the financial
advantage of the church's holdings.

Noonan also opposes any correlation between scholastic economic analysis and those, like R. H. Tawney, who would use it in
support of the labor theory of value. Noonan writes, "The whole
scholastic attitude towards the *societas* is refutation of Tawney's
rash assertion, 'The true descendant of the doctrines of Aquinas
is the labor theory of value. The last of the Schoolmen was Karl
Marx'" (Noonan, 1957, 152). Although Tawney's statement does lack
sufficient warrant, Noonan himself may be a bit rash in dismissing Tawney's analysis. To be sure, the scholastics had no notion of
a labor theory of value as a social-scientific account of what gives
commodities value. If that is the connection Tawney sought to
make, Noonan is correct in dismissing him. Nevertheless, Tawney
does recognize that any discussion of scholastic economics, and
especially the usury theory, must be done in the context of "the sin
of avarice," which is the name of the chapter from which Noonan
draws the infamous Tawney quote.

Medieval economics cannot be understood without recognizing the threat avarice posed to the social, political, and religious
order. Noonan seldom mentions this in his efforts to read the usury
prohibition solely in terms of the natural law. However, Tawney

rightly recognized how a different politics is required to understand the scholastics position from the modern one, an analysis
that requires a different conception of labor, wages, and prices than
modern economics tolerates. Tawney stated, "The medieval theo-
rist condemned as a sin precisely that effort to achieve a continuous
and unlimited increase in material wealth which modern societies applaud as a quality . . ." (Tawney, 1954, 38). Tawney overstates
his argument when he proclaims Marx as the "last of the schoolmen." Marx never considered economics in terms of holiness, sin,
and the theological virtues and vices. He was thoroughly modern
in that he thought he was offering us an objective social scientific
analysis. However, as Odd Langholm and Alasdair MacIntyre have
shown, the scholastics consistently affirmed a connection between
one's labor and an appropriate remuneration. Langholm calls this a
"'political' labor theory" rather than one of "value."[27] Nevertheless,
Tawney's attribution of Marx as a Thomist, and Noonan's dismissal
of Tawney's claim, reveals how various contemporary political and
economic movements find in the scholastics anticipations of their
positions even when they seek to just give us the historical facts.

    Another such use of the usury prohibition is found in the econ-
omist, John Maynard Keynes's *General Theory of Employment, Interest
and Money*. He wrote,

> I was brought up to believe that the attitude of the Medieval
> Church to the rate of interest was inherently absurd, and that the
> subtle discussions aimed at distinguishing the return on money-
> loans from the return to active investment was merely Jesuiti-
> cal attempts to find a practical escape from a foolish theory. But
> I now read these discussions as an honest intellectual effort to
> keep separate what the classical theory has inextricably confused
> together, namely, the rate of interest and the marginal efficiency
> of capital. For it now seems clear that the disquisitions of the
> schoolmen were directed towards the elucidation of a formula

which should allow the schedule of marginal efficiency of capital
to be high, whilst using rule and custom and the moral law to
keep down the rate of interest. (Keynes, 1964, 351–52)

He may be one of the first modern economists who drew upon the
scholastic analysis as anticipatory of modern economics rather than
opposed to it. It sparked a response by a number of persons—some
who dismissed Keynes for reviving the old usury analysis at all. Others defended it, but against Keynes' employment of it. Such were
the feelings of the Jesuit economist, Bernard Dempsey, who trained
under Joseph Schumpeter.

The anticipatory interpretation of the usury prohibition reads
an inevitable progress from the efforts of the scholastics to modern
economics. But, in a way it does not for modern economics, this
ignores the fact that theology mattered for the scholastic analysis.
Joan Lockwood O'Donovan recognizes that Langholm tends to lose
this "theological complexity" which assumed a "Christocentric ethics of perfection" (O'Donovan, 2004, 98).

Noonan reminds us that we will not be able to understand well
the usury prohibition if we ignore its theological foundation. "What
mattered for the Scholastics," he writes, "was the biblical, patristic
and conciliar texts which had been taken as decisive by medieval
pontiffs and councils" (Noonan, 1957, 12–13). Noonan recognizes
that theological dogma renders the usury prohibition intelligible
even when modified by late scholasticism to allow for more and
more exceptions. Even these exceptions are not an unequivocal
capitulation to modern economics. Noonan rejects a thoroughgoing accommodationist thesis that "ascribes" these exceptions "to
the emancipated reason celebrated by the later liberals" (Noonan,
1957, 399). These claims could lead us to think Noonan rejected any
anticipatory interpretation of usury altogether. That would be mistaken, however. He interprets the scholastic analysis as "Western
man's first try at an economic theory." And he certainly finds the
later medieval theory preferable to earlier because later medieval

theory "is modified by writers appealing frankly to nature and reason against the past" (Noonan, 1957, 398).

As the usury prohibition becomes based more on "natural law" and "reason" apart from more specific theological resources, it becomes more reasonable. It is no surprise then that Cardinal Cajetan, who developed a doctrine of humanity's double finality, plays such a positive role in Noonan's telling of the story.[28]

Like Noonan, it would be improper to read Langholm's important work simply as anticipatory of modern capitalism. Nevertheless, he himself claims that an "anticipatory" approach animates his work, and this does seem to force his analysis into thoroughly modern categories. He views scholastic economic ethics as "the conflict between the Christian deontology inherited from the patristic tradition and the Christian utilitarianism forced upon the medieval scholastics by social and economic change" (Langholm, 1992, 9). Do these modern ethical categories make sense for patristic and scholastic economics? For Langholm, utilitarianism inevitably wins out. This occurs as scholastic economics moves out of its theological matrix in the penitential tradition and into a more universal notion of rationality grounded in the natural law. Langholm writes, "Scholastic economics may well be said to have been born by canon law and tended at first in the penitential, but it soon outgrew its cradle" (Langholm, 1992, 63). Only as scholastic economics becomes planted "on a broad basis extending from theology into law—and in fact beyond law into classical moral philosophy" does it have a lasting power. For Langholm, the recovery of Aristotle's moral teachings provides the broader basis that makes for the usury prohibitions ongoing relevance.[29]

### THE USURY PROHIBITION AS THE "THIRD WAY"

Does something like scholastic economic analysis and the usury prohibition provide a "third way" beyond capitalism and socialism? From Leo XIII's *Rerum Novarum* to Pius XI's *Quadragesimo Anno*,

Catholic social teaching suggested a possible economic alternative to both capitalism and socialism, which was related to the usury prohibition. For as Leo XIII stated, "voracious usury" was practiced by "avaricious men" in late nineteenth-century industrial capitalism.[30] *Quadragesimo Anno* and the encyclical tradition in Catholic teaching is an effort to chart a third way that deals with the lingering problem of "voracious usury" grounded in the vice of "avarice." Seldom is it, however, that "avarice" appears in discussions of usury or in Catholic or Protestant economic ethics. Instead, we seem to have been preoccupied with defending either capitalism or socialism. Some claim capitalism itself to be the "third way." It is consistent with Catholic social teaching and so we need not look for any "reconstruction of the social order." As Michael Novak put it, "There are no existing examples of the Catholic middle way. Catholic social teaching has, therefore, occupied a sort of utopian ground—literally no place. It came to seem uncharacteristically abstract, otherworldly, deracinated" (Novak, 1982, 247–48). While some find capitalism to be the only faithful option, others, especially liberation theologians, continue to look to socialism as that which best makes sense of Catholic social teaching. The debate between these two sides has so preoccupied contemporary Christian ethics that it tended to neglect the efforts of others who tried to find a third way by drawing upon traditional Catholic teaching and applying it to modern economics. One such person was the Jesuit Bernard Dempsey with his efforts to set forth a "functional economy."

Dempsey's functional economy was no revolutionary ethic. As he explained it, the functional economy "projects the ideal situation, which intelligent adherence to the enlightened teachings of the Church and constant awareness of the lessons of history can achieve, against the background of historic and existing economic communities" (Dempsey, 1958, i). However, this functional economy does not require a break with traditional teaching. It assumes that "long before 1600 entirely sound principles had been formulated on prices, values, money, usury, risk and interest, inflation, taxation, private property and the division of labor" (Dempsey, 1958, 4). Such principles were both continuous and discontinuous with modern economics. Nevertheless, for Dempsey these principles fit best with Schumpeter's economic analysis.[31]

In his *Interest and Usury*, Dempsey correlates scholastic teaching with modern economics. He finds Knut Wicksell's account of interest preferable because it recognized a relationship between money and a natural propensity for goods to reproduce. "If goods did not have the characteristic of producing a greater volume of goods in time," Dempsey argued, "interest as a production factor would not exist" (Dempsey, 1943, 26). Dempsey may be one of the last defenders of something like Aristotle's sterility argument. Like Noonan and Langholm, he tends to understand scholastic economics in terms of Cajetan's double finality. Thus, he can speak about economic matters solely in terms of nature without any specific references to grace or the theological virtues.[32] However, this has produced significant problems in Catholic social teaching. As long as economic analysis is done in terms of Cajetan's distorted Thomism with its double finality, the specific role of the church, and its importance for the economy, will be neglected. We will falsely think we can cling to the tradition of moral theology—without the theology—and with no reference to ecclesiology.

VIRTUE AS THAT WHICH RENDERS INTELLIGIBLE THE USURY PROHIBITION

The usury prohibition, as well as other key elements of scholastic economics, is not a global economic system that all persons could adhere to irrespective of their theological commitments. If that is what social justice requires, then the church's traditional teaching will most likely not have much to say to modern economic institutions. To attempt to turn this command into such a system would be to misunderstand the tradition of moral theology that renders intelligible the usury prohibition. Instead of seeking to find in it a blueprint for a universal economic system, an Enlightenment endeavor we no longer need to pursue, the virtue tradition of Thomas Aquinas can help us understand the contemporary social and political significance of the usury prohibition. For Aquinas, law directs human acts to virtuous ends. The law is not intelligible in itself, but it fits within a teleological ordering of human existence that seeks the excellences we call virtues—including the theological virtue of charity. The end of human existence is friendship with God. Virtues allow us to participate in the divine life; they draw us into God's own being. Without such an account of virtue, law can only appear arbitrary. I think this is what happened in the history of the usury prohibition; it no longer made sense once money was not considered to have a teleological ordering toward Christ.

Once we see that usury is not necessarily exploitative, but as Calvin and late scholastics argued, usurious exchanges can be mutually beneficial in utilitarian terms, then on what grounds might we object to them? Especially once charity is understood not as a virtue by which we participate in the divine life (2 Pet 1:4), but merely in the modern terms of an exchange that benefits the participants. What is wrong with the unlimited growth of money producing more money? Only if we have a robust doctrine of holiness, where the Christian life is a journey to cultivate those virtues by which God intends us to live, mediated through Christ and the church, can the usury prohibition make sense.

Aquinas' treatment of usury in his *De malo* helps us understand how virtues and vices render the usury prohibition intelligible. He is not directly offering us a social or political theology, but explaining how to avoid evil and pursue good which for Aquinas, like Aristotle, was the fundamental political question. This question then requires social and political theology that understands what the good is and how evil is to be avoided. The seven "capital" vices are the fount from which all other vices flow. Note the language used for them; they are capital. This is because, like capital, they appear to increase without recognizing any proper limits. All the capital vices are parodies of proper human desires because they assume an infinite expansion of finite goods. If we fail to recognize how capital vices function, we will miss why Aquinas opposes usury. In fact, his argument against usury does not come until question thirteen of the *De malo* after he first develops his doctrine of evil. While evil alone cannot explain the usury prohibition, this is an essential theological point found in the *De malo*. Good, not evil, defines the created order. Therefore, if anyone says he can find good in usury then Aquinas would not object because he says as much himself. It is part of his larger ontological claim, "Evil cannot exist except in good."[33] Radical evil, the kind of evil Kant made famous, does not exist for Aquinas.[34] For this reason, a certain taxonomy of virtues and vices must first be recognized before Aquinas' prohibition of usury makes sense. First come the virtues of charity, justice, and liberality. Then comes the lack of these three virtues in the "capital" vice of avarice. This lack manifests itself in different degrees so that avarice as a defect of liberality is not a mortal sin, but avarice as a defect of charity or justice is.

Four articles make up question thirteen of *De malo*. Is avarice a special vice? (That is, does it have a specific subject matter or only a generic one?) The second question is if it is a mortal sin followed by questioning whether it is a capital vice. Only after establishing this context does Aquinas address the fourth question "Is lending at usury a mortal sin?"

Aquinas argues that avarice is a *special sin*, even though it is not contrary to only one thing. This argument objects to Aristotle, who argued in book 10 of the *Metaphysics* that a vice is "special" or "specific" only if it opposes one thing, but avarice is opposed to charity, justice, and liberty. Therefore, how can it be a special sin?[35] Aquinas' response is that avarice is a specific vice because, at one level it, "signifies an inordinate desire of money." Money provides it with a "special kind of matter." The misuse of money constitutes the sin of avarice specifically. Yet, Aquinas also finds it a general sin. He writes, "because of a certain likeness this name [avarice] has been extended to signify an inordinate cupidity or desire of any goods whatsoever. And in this sense avarice is a general sin, because in every sin there is a turning to some transitory good with inordinate desire; and therefore Augustine says that there is a general avarice by which a person desires anything more than he ought, and there is a special avarice which more commonly is called love of money" (*De malo* 13.1; Aquinas, 1993). The specific threat of an inordinate desire of money and the generic inordinate cupidity "of any goods whatsoever" mutually reinforce each other. Avarice then designates one specific thing—an inordinate love of money—and more than one thing. In fact, it can designate an improper desire for all created goods. It is not merely a disposition, but more a corrupt practice of the use of money that "unnaturally" increases it through an acquisitiveness that turns all finite goods into the source of an infinite desire.

Avarice then does not oppose a single virtue. It opposes the virtues of charity, justice, and liberality. It opposes liberality when "avarice signifies a certain defect in regard to the dispensing of wealth and a certain excess in regard to its acquisition and retention because of an excessive love of money." Here some refuse to give even when justice does not demand it. This is not a mortal sin. It opposes justice when, as Aristotle taught, one "takes or keeps another's goods contrary to the debt of justice." This is a mortal sin. And it opposes charity because it finds happiness in the mere increase of a created good rather than in the uncreated good, which God is. Aquinas sums this up: "Avarice is opposed to justice and to liberality according to the diverse senses or interpretations of avarice, but it is opposed to charity as is every mortal sin, inasmuch as it constitutes a created good as its end" (*De malo* 13.1 rep. 7; Aquinas, 1993).

Avarice and its vicious practice in usury is, therefore, a complex reality. It has degrees of evil which, as Thomas already noted, will always be related to good. If we do not understand this, we will be confused as to the *casuistic* nature of medieval moral theology. It is not an inevitable accommodation to market realities but a prudent analysis of the levels of virtue and vice and how they do and do not direct our desires to God. If we do not have an account of these virtues and vices, the usury prohibition appears as a silly legalism. Central to these virtues and vices is the telos of happiness. Our lives make sense in terms of their true end in friendship with God.

The seven capital sins are so dangerous because they trade on that very end. Aquinas explains the capital sins this way: "Therefore those vices are called capital which have ends principally desirable in themselves in such a way that other vices are ordered to these ends" (*De malo* 18.1; Aquinas, 1993). Capital vices are like usurious exchanges. Both become ends in themselves to which other aspects of our lives get ordered. They function as a false happiness because they produce infinite desire for finite goods.

Aquinas explicitly names avarice as a capital vice because it is ordered to a false happiness.

> Avarice ought to be counted among the capital vices. The reason for this is that, as was said previously, a vice is called capital that has a principal end to which many other vices are naturally ordered, and thus by way of final causality many other vices have their origin from such a vice. But the end or goal of the whole of human life is happiness which all men desire; hence inasmuch as in human affairs something participates really or apparently in any condition of happiness, happiness has a certain pre-eminence in the genus of ends. But there are three conditions of happiness according to the Philosopher in Book I of the Ethics, namely that it be a perfect good and sufficient of itself (per se) and accompanied by pleasure. Now a thing seems to be perfect inasmuch as it has a certain excellence, and therefore excellence seems to be something principally desirable, and in accord with this, pride or vainglory is designated as a capital vice; and in sensed things the most intense pleasure has to do with the sense of touch in food

or sex, and therefore gluttony and lust are designated as capital
vices; moreover a sufficiency of temporal goods is assured chiefly
by money, as Boethius says in Book II and Book III On the Consola-
tion of Philosophy, hence avarice, which is an inordinate desire
of riches, also must be counted as a capital vice. (De malo 13.3;
Aquinas, 1993)

Thomas begins by recognizing the role of happiness and desire in
the moral life; it does not exist without them. Happiness is characterized in Aristotelian terms as "a perfect good," "sufficient of
itself," and "accompanied by pleasure." False happiness also trades
on these three characteristics. Pride, gluttony, lust, and avarice all
present themselves with these three characteristics; they are all
parodies of true happiness. Pride does this with immaterial goods.
Gluttony, lust, and avarice do it with material goods. Once these
vices become ends in themselves, and thus they are capital vices,
then they produce other vices that are necessary to order one's
life toward this false happiness. Thomas, drawing on Gregory the
Great's Moralia, "assigns seven daughters" to avarice, "which are
treachery, fraud, deceit, perjury, restlessness, violence, obduracy in
regard to mercy."

More so than Aristotle's sterility argument or natural law per
se, Aquinas' prohibition of usury assumes this complex of virtues—
charity, justice, and liberality—and vices—avarice with its seven
daughters. This occurs when money becomes an end in itself. It is
a false happiness. Money must serve other ends not because of a
specific economic analysis of how money functions, but because of
Aquinas' theological claims about what constitutes true human happiness. This does not mean that we can say, as Margaret Thatcher
said in 1988, "It is not the creation of wealth that is wrong but love
of money for its own sake" (Buckley, 2000, 319). For Aquinas, avarice
is not an internal disposition that is irrelevant to how we exchange
and use the money. How wealth is created will be a matter of char-

ity, justice, liberality, or avarice. Wealth creation itself matters. Aquinas' usury analysis helps us discern to which of these we are and are not ordered. What "capital" funds our life? If we think that our money can simply work for us, can increase without industry, and increase without its proper teleological ordering, then we will be funded by avarice. What is interesting is that the very kind of false happiness Aquinas warns us of in *De malo* seems to me to be precisely what J. S. Mill and the liberal economic tradition of utilitarianism advocates—desire growth without limit through mutual optimizing of utility.

Why does this matter? To locate Aquinas' teaching on usury within the context of happiness and the virtues is to offer an analysis very different from most of the classical treatments. Those who interpret the usury prohibition as anticipatory of modern capitalism or of the labor theory of value do so by finding in it a concern only for justice grounded in natural law. Some who interpret it as a third way do so only in terms of its potential for a universal economic policy. Those who interpret it as an irrational dogmatic attachment to positive authority or as a medieval deontology miss the different social framework that divides modern economics from scholastic economics. Even accounts of greed that argue the love of money is vicious, still acknowledge that we can be involved in any kind of economic exchange we desire as long as we are not too attached to our money and miss altogether the importance of virtue and vice.

Alasdair MacIntyre notes how it was Hobbes who first interpreted the Aristotelian vice of *pleonexia* as merely "a desire for more than [one's] share." However, MacIntyre suggests, this is an incorrect understanding of this vice. Therefore, English translations of Aristotle's *Nichomachean Ethics,* such as Irwin's, which translate pleonexia as greed and understand it as primarily a disposition to have more than one's share, miss the point. *Pleonexia*, like avarice, is a vice that—from a specific sociality—always demands more. MacIntyre writes:

What such translations of "pleonexia" conceal from us is the extent of the difference between Aristotle's standpoint on the virtues and vices, and more especially his standpoint on justice and the dominant standpoint of peculiarly modern societies. For the adherents of that standpoint recognize that acquisitiveness is a character trait indispensable to continuous and limitless economic growth, and one of their central beliefs is that continuous and limitless economic growth is a fundamental good. That a systematically lower standard of living ought to be preferred to a systematically higher standard of living is a thought incompatible with either the economics or the politics of peculiarly modern societies. So prices and wages have come to be understood as unrelated—and indeed in a modern economy could not be related—to desert in terms of labor, and the notion of a just price or a just wage in modern terms makes no sense. But a community which was guided by Aristotelian norms would not only have to view acquisitiveness as a vice but would have to set strict limits to growth as that is necessary to preserve or enhance a distribution of goods according to desert. (MacIntyre, 1988, 111–12)

As MacIntyre notes, the fundamental problem with modern capitalist economics is that it has no place for merit. One's labor and wages bear little to no connection to each other. But the usury prohibition, grounded in the virtues of charity, justice, and liberality, could only function well within an economy where such connections exist.

Aquinas' avarice and Aristotle's pleonexia help us make sense of the usury prohibition. Of course, they both understood that it does appear money can increase without limit. They recognized that someone could loan money and receive a perpetual return. However, this very reality was an evil because it was an increase that knew no limits. It was desire for desire's sake. It was money as raw power. Once this occurred desire loses its proper end; in fact, it becomes endless. But since nothing finite is endless, this produces vice. The ability to be bound by such a boundless vice disorders social and political reality. This requires a constant vigilance to insure our lives are not bound by such acquisitiveness for its own sake. How do we know when our end has become this capital vice?

The usury prohibition is not a single rule to be applied indiscriminately across times and places; it is not Kant's categorical imperative. It is a rule that requires prudence to apply it properly. This is a function of practical reason that needs a communal context in order to work it out; it requires a community on a quest for holiness that is capable of and knows how to confess its sins. The proper social location for the usury prohibition is not the state, civil society, or any kind of blueprint for a universal economic system. It is first and foremost the confessional. If there is no global Christian community seeking holiness by recognizing the vice of pleonexia as well as the virtues of charity and justice, then the Christian usury prohibition will make no sense. However, such communities do exist and they hold forth the possibility of alternative forms of banking, of corporate life, and of forms of exchange that may never produce a single global economic system that insures justice for all. Yet, they can advance and can help us remember that peculiar notion of justice that can be found in our faith traditions.

# — 7 —

## A CATHOLIC CHURCH AND GLOBAL MARKET

## The Tale of Two Corporations

Does the social justice required to sustain the usury prohibition and the virtue to which it points provide an alternative to the question whether Christians must be socialists or capitalists? The account of theological economics presented in the previous chapter can only make sense in terms of those Christian doctrines that make charity essential to proper human flourishing. This entails that theologians, even when commenting on economic matters, do so primarily as theologians. We should not expect them to be social scientists; they will never do that well. We should expect them to be theologians. This will make us as concerned to show how Christian doctrine matters for our economic exchanges as a concern to defend some global economic system. Too much of theological reflection on economics has been preoccupied with whether we must be socialists or capitalists.

Must the church decide which global economic system it should support? Does it have a stake in the question: shall we be socialists or capitalists? To continue to ask these questions at the beginning of the twenty-first century can only appear antiquated, for despite the attention theologians gave to these questions in the nineteenth and twentieth centuries, they now appear settled. Whether we lament or celebrate events that transpired since 1989, Michael Novak seems descriptively accurate when he tells us, "We are all capitalists now, even the Pope. Both traditionalist and socialist methods have failed; for the whole world there is now only one form of economics" (Novak, 1993, 101). Some celebrate this as the "end of history" and the "triumph of the VCR," while others lament it as the "end of modernity," which does not designate a completed state, but a state that can never be completed, only endlessly repeated. The "new and improved" becomes our fate, for the critical frame of mind capitalism requires sets itself against all things traditional, even those that were transmitted only a short time ago.[36] Everything must be new; everything must be freed.

Whether someone celebrates the triumph of capitalism as the end of history or laments it as the endless end of modernity, the questions with which this chapter began can only appear—at this moment in history—as anachronistic. The question is already answered. "We are all capitalists now," if not in theory then at least in practice. And yet the fact that many contemporary theologians continue to proclaim capitalism's triumph betrays theologians' lingering preoccupation with this question of which global economic system we should construct, a preoccupation that is dangerous for two related reasons. First, to announce the triumph of a specific global economic system tacitly assumes and affirms the competence of theologians to make determinations about which global system of exchange should rule over us. But this is both a competence and a form of rule that theologians cannot possess as theologians. Such a claim requires theologians to present themselves as expert social scientists or at least to subordinate theological dogma to the expertise of the social sciences in order to occupy a space where this question can be asked and answered. Second, by seeking to make theology relevant by occupying this space, theologians contribute to their own irrelevance and to the increasing marginalization of theology, particularly dogma. For theology's irrelevance is part of the end of history and the end of modernity. At either end, theology does not matter. No legitimation for any global economic system is needed from the church, its theologians, or its philosopher.

As Jean-François Lyotard has persuasively argued, the state of modern knowledge, with its technological preoccupation and its rigid focus on efficiency, does not need any legitimating discourse; it is self-legitimating solely on the pragmatic grounds that "it works." Both philosophy and theology become, at best, like works of art in a museum to be gazed at by intellectual connoisseurs. In such a time as this the question, "Which global economic system should the Church, its theologians, and its philosophers support?" would be like asking, "How can we reconstruct the medieval guild system?" The question makes no sense; answering it can have no meaning. Yet, seriously asking the question and providing an answer can only increase theology's irrelevance, for it assumes that what is real—the standard of measurement against which theology is to be assessed—is a global economic system that is self-legitimating.

In fact, the present historical moment presents an opportunity for theology to recover its specific task. No longer must theologians be obsessed with modernist accommodations, asking ourselves how we can make theology relevant to those disciplines—in particular the social sciences—that seek to present and sell themselves as offering the expertise necessary to navigate the pragmatic corridors of meaning that rule the present age. Theology, especially moral theology, has for too long been a pale imitation of social science. By recognizing that these disciplines need no legitimation—philosophically or theologically—theologians become free to do what theology does, which is to speak well about God. We are freed at the end of modernity to pursue the dogmatic task that is theology.

Theology cannot be theology without this dogmatic task being its center. That task is to explain in each generation how irreversible decisions by those who came before us give us the language that allows us to speak well of God. Theology's sole task is to show how dogmas—which are rooted in Scripture, elucidated in conciliar decisions, and further clarified by the faithful, pastors, and theologians, train us in speaking about God such that God's name—and, thus, how we are to live—will not be forgotten. For theologians to begin by claiming competence in those disciplines that claim responsibility for global economic systems is already to begin at the wrong point. We must begin with God; that is what makes us "theologians." And all knowledge of God comes as a gift mediated to us from the witnesses who preceded us. If we are to be theologians, then, our first task is the dogmatic task. And related to that dogmatic task is the doctrinal task of envisioning the world, including the world of economic exchange, in terms of the church's teachings. In this essay I will claim the only competence I know—that of being a theologian. I will perform the theologian's task by telling a tale of two corporations and then discerning how theologians can respond to them by the dogmas and teachings they use or fail to use. I hope this approach will ask the proper theological question, "How are we to be faithful in these times, which we must discern by the gift of dogma and doctrine handed down to us?"

### A Tale of Two Corporations

To read economics theologically is within the proper competence of the theologian. To read theology through the lens of an economist is not. To do the first, limits the kind of questions that can be meaningfully asked, but it does not limit the kind of activities to which theology must be mediated. As Scripture and tradition unmistakably demonstrate, nothing is more theological than everyday economic exchanges. They must be read theologically. Before pursuing the dogmatic task, which is to assess critically the dogma and doctrines theologians use to help us read economic exchanges theologically, some concrete examples of economic exchanges within modern corporations will be presented. I will begin by narrating the story of two corporations. The first corporation is so unjust that it is a rather easy case; it is difficult to defend. Although, as mentioned earlier, Bandow offers a partial defense of it. The second corporation is a much more difficult case. It is not obviously exploitative and, in fact, does tremendous good in the local community in which its plant has been located since the corporation's inception. By narrating the story of these two corporations, I hope to help think through the differences theology might make for understanding economic exchanges. These descriptions are not intended to be social-scientific analyses; they are, at best, biographical narrations that I hope readers will find persuasive as reasonable accounts of economic exchange in the modern corporation. The first corporation is an arm of a multinational that prepares shrimp and lobster from the waters off the coast of Honduras for fast-food consumption in the United States. The second is a local, family-owned corporation primarily confined to one small city in the Midwest.

The lobster and shrimp plant is found in Honduras. The women who worked in the plant processing lobster and shrimp were primarily Guarifuna—an African people brought to Latin America during the Middle Passage who had rebelled against their slave owners, established a village off the north coast of Honduras, and maintained their traditional African customs for five hundred years. The Guarifuna lived in a village several miles from the plant. The men would do the lobstering; they were often at sea for weeks and months at a time. The women would process the lobster and shrimp. They were paid seventy-five cents per hour for their work, and they worked as long as work was available—anywhere from six to twelve hours a day, once the lobster and shrimp arrived. There were no unions, no labor contracts, no health care, and no enforceable laws pertaining to working conditions. The transportation of the lobster and shrimp to the (primarily American) market was a lucrative business for the few Hondurans who owned the processing plant and the shipping vessels. The disparity in living conditions between these ship owners and the workers was obvious. No social science was necessary to see it. All one had to do was open one's eyes, walk through the two villages in which the Guarifuna and the owners lived, and compare them. The Guarifuna village had no running water, no electricity, no paved roads, and most homes were mud constructions with thatched roofs. The owners of the plant and ships had running water and electricity and their homes were modern constructions capable of withstanding the gale force winds that often hit the island. Many of them also had second homes in the United States.

The wages paid to the men who secured the lobster and shrimp (often by diving without gear to dangerous ocean depths) and the women who processed them were insufficient to purchase the product they themselves produced. At seventy-five cents per hour, assuming a fifty-hour workweek, the weekly pay would be $37.50. A five-pound box of lobster would be sold for nearly half that amount. In other words, the very men and women who risked securing and processing this food, the men and women whose hands were the conditions for making lobster and shrimp available as consumable food items for others, were then excluded from consuming the produce they made available. Others profited more from their labor than they did, which is a clear sign of avarice.

This was (and is) an unjust situation. I hope no theologian would intentionally defend these kinds of exploitative practices; for, insofar as God and Scripture still matter, these practices cannot be justified. Every theologian, who is not simply an ideologue, must recognize that such unjust practices do occur and object to them because they are sinful, and God is against sin. But have theologians given us the language to explain why these practices are objectionable? What difference does their theology make? How do dogmas and doctrines help us name these practices? This is the dogmatic task appropriate to theologians.

Before more fully pursuing that dogmatic task, I need to accomplish two things. First, I want to avoid any suggestion that I have offered a neutral social analysis of "reality." Second, I will present a more positive modern corporation so that I do not gain an unfair rhetorical advantage by taking this lobster and shrimp plant as the only form of capitalist exchange. Both of these corporations function within the present global economic system. Which of them fits more easily within that system, and which is an aberration, remains an open question.

My description of the shrimp and lobster corporation as "corrupt" is not based on the secure deliverances of some "abstract" universal reason, be it a "natural" law or an objective analysis of "social" reality qua "social" disembodied from a particular tradition. It is grounded in a confessional claim about who God is. That is what makes it theological. This confessional claim is also unavoidable. Moral theologians' efforts to avoid such confessions lead to ironic claims about what they are doing—claims that neglect the conditions that make their work possible. My own conclusion will be that the true social descriptions I have given depend upon Christology, ecclesiology, and the doctrine of the Trinity. Moral theologians on both the political Left and Right object to this dogmatic approach, apparently because it hampers their ability to speak publicly. Thus, "natural law," the doctrine of creation, an "incarnational" (as opposed to the Incarnation), or a "sacramental" (as opposed to the sacraments) approach seems to be the order of the day. Why Christology and ecclesiology are too confessionally oriented—but something like creation is not—mystifies me. For to speak of "creation" is already to make a confession standing within a particular tradition, and if that tradition is Christian then one cannot speak of creation without its Christological and Trinitarian resonances. Creation is not a more universal category than Christology or Trinity. They render it intelligible.

The example of the shrimp and lobster plant is much too easy. For those of us who stand within the Christian tradition, it is obviously wicked. Using it as the only example of economic exchange would be uncharitable, for not every form of economic exchange in the modern corporation functions in this way. *Abusus non tollit usum.*

A much more positive tale of a corporation concerns a water meter factory that, like many such corporations, plays an integral function within the life of a small midwestern town. This corporation is not publicly traded; the stock is held by one family—all of whose members live in the community where the plant operates. It is a non-union plant, yet many decisions are made collectively. Profits are shared based on annual productivity and, in an economic downturn, the workers and owners together decide if a reduction in wages or layoffs are necessary. The family who owns the plant is well known for its frugality as well as its members' contributions to the common good of the local community. The family lives in and among the persons who work for the plant. It has used the profits it has accrued from owning the plant to establish a number of endowments that support local young people in their college education or in their pursuit of the arts. Local workers have long sought the coveted jobs at the factory precisely because the family can be trusted. Key to this trust is the family's commitment to their local church, which is reflected in how they operate the plant.

It seems inconceivable for this factory to move from its location in the small Midwestern town where it is located, but it remains a possibility since the excellent relationship between workers and owners depends on the family's commitments to church and place. Ownership is transferred biologically. What happens if the next generation does not share these commitments? What happens if the moral and legal imperative to maximize profits becomes more decisive than the family's traditional commitments? Given the legal and moral nature of the modern corporation, is it inevitable that in order to survive this corporation will eventually be forced to forego these commitments?[37]

Which of these two corporations is more normative within the current context within which modern corporations operate? If the primary task of the corporation is to maximize profits based on the legal protections afforded by limited liability, then surely it is the lobster/shrimp plant. If the primary task of the corporation is to be understood in theological terms, then perhaps it is the water meter plant.

How should we assess corporations theologically? The descriptions I have offered are, and should be, contested. No single satisfying explanation of the reality of the exchanges that take place in these corporations is possible. Thus, I think it unreasonable to assume that a "rational analysis of social reality" qua reason alone will be able to adjudicate the contending descriptions. Neither do I think we must resolve the issue politically, where politics is understood primarily in terms of power. As theologians, we must be ruled by our inheritance, by how we have learned to speak well of God. Truth and goodness must be more basic to our work than the will to power. We must have the kind of conversation within our competence as theologians and people of faith that could, in fact, provide a reasonable basis in which to answer the question of what our theological tradition has to say about these two corporations and the kinds of practices they embody. Which dogmas matter, and why?

### The Dogmatic Task

Every theologian should recognize that participation in the modern corporation is not a priori evil; it can be a faithful form of discipleship. In fact, economic exchanges are necessary for everyday life; we must have them, and corporations make them possible. The dogmatic question is what constitutes faithful participation in these forms of exchange. Some theologians find the modern corporation central not only to everyday exchange but also to God's economy itself. Michael Novak finds the modern corporation to be an "incarnation" of God's presence, and an institution that has something like a sacramental mission. Dennis McCann and Max Stackhouse speak of it as a "worldly ecclesia." Gustavo Gutiérrez, like most liberation theologians, does not attribute this kind of incarnational presence to the modern corporation, but like Novak, McCann, and

Stackhouse he finds God working in an autonomous political realm without ecclesial mediation. Gutiérrez finds "the frontiers between the life of faith and temporal works, between Church and world," to be "fluid" such that participation in a more secular process of liberation would be participation in "a salvific work." (Gutiérrez, 1993, 45–46) The corporation is neither an incarnation nor a worldly ecclesia for Gutiérrez, but the "process of liberation" is. If corporations participated in that process, then they might have the status afforded them by Novak, McCann, and Stackhouse. John Milbank and Alasdair MacInytre offer a different theological (and philosophical) approach to thinking about the corporation. They do not accept the secularization thesis implicitly and explicitly present in the above theologians. Instead, they narrate the history within which the modern corporation has emerged and suggest that this history is itself already a theological distortion, even a heretical inheritance. Thus, the modern corporation is a danger to faith that needs the guidance of the church's teaching office (at least for MacIntyre) if we are not to lose our souls to it.

### The Heretical Status of Capitalist Exchanges

Gustavo Gutiérrez associates the process of liberation with socialism. "Faith and political action will not enter into a correct and fruitful relationship except through the effort to create a new type of person in a different society." That "different society," he speaks of must be socialist. Only a socialist society would allow for the flourishing of the human person consistent with Christian principles. Yet, he does not reach this conclusion (one with which John Milbank agrees) through the dogmatic task of the theologian. For Gutiérrez, this different society is not primarily an ecclesial work. It is to be accomplished, rather, by "respecting the autonomy of the political arena," and thus, Gutiérrez's affirmation of socialism is not primarily theological, but arises out of an "effective . . . rational analysis of reality" (Gutiérrez, 1993, 138). It does not finally grant sufficient place for what theologians do; instead, it allows for an autonomous political realm known primarily through the mediation of the social sciences. The socialist vision is not dependent on church teaching. In fact, Gutiérrez finds liberation theology preferable to much that is in Catholic social thought because liberation theology takes more seriously the kind of careful social analysis that does not shy away from speaking of the class conflict endemic to capitalism, a conflict that is a "social fact."[38]

Milbank agrees with Gutiérrez that Christian faith requires socialist forms of economic exchange and the abolition of capitalism. However, he refutes Gutiérrez's claim that this conclusion can be reached by way of a "rational analysis of reality," for no such analysis exists. No social fact exists because the social is not subject to explanation but only narration. There is no neutral and universal explanatory mechanism grounded in laws governing natural causality within social systems. Every account of the social is always historically mediated. Milbank finds that the very universal and neutral reading of social reality found in the social sciences already has within it heretical dogmatic commitments.

> If theology accepts modern liberal economics at their own evaluation, then it has, in reality, already made decisions within theology itself, and has endorsed a whole series of buried infinities between the modern scientific approach to politics and economics and the fideist-nominalist-voluntarist current in theology which is inherited, through seventeenth-century writers like Hobbes and Grotius, from the late Middle Ages. The shortest route to unraveling the problem of theology and economics is to become aware of this history. It is within voluntarist theology that the key philosophy of "possessive individualism" has is origins. *Jus* (right) is first thought of as dominium or as power over property within a perspective which understood God's creative activity and relation to the world in terms of an arbitrary exercise of power. (Milbank, 1986, 39)

The abolition of capitalism has a quasi-dogmatic status in Milbank's work only because its emergence had such a status. To be for capitalism is already to side with certain heretical theological options against the orthodox, dogmatic tradition.

For Milbank, the Christian opposition to capitalism arises solely for theological reasons. The gift God exchanges with creation through Christ must be the basis of all exchanges. Christianity opposes capitalism because the gift can never be reduced to a contract with nicely calculated profit/loss ratios where individuals enter into exchanges without being fundamentally changed by those exchanges. The Christian life requires a gift economy in which a return is always expected—as it should be when one gives gifts—but never one that can be calculated such that the contract terminates and the relationship dissolves. This approaches more closely what Oliver O'Donovan refers to as "communication." Instead of what we exchange freeing us from each other (as is the case with contracts in capitalist exchanges, in which everyone's fate—including that of the corporation—is to be a free autonomous individual), our exchanges should take us ever more deeply into a "mutual but asymmetrical reciprocity." For this reason, Milbank states, "we must have a socialist market. We must strive still to abolish capitalism, albeit this must now be undertaken on a global scale and must often work within businesses, seeking to turn them into primarily socially responsible and not profit seeking organizations" (Milbank, 1996, 544). To say we must work within businesses recognizes their legitimacy. But how do we transform them from within? Milbank invites Christians to see their work, exchanges, and ownership within the context of what it means to be church. The corporation does not replace the church as a form of the body of Christ; instead, it gains its intelligibility within the life of the church—especially the church's liturgical performance.

According to Milbank, capitalism not only emerges out of a reaction against the orthodox, dogmatic tradition, it is sustained by a "Weberian resigned acceptance of the fatalities of power"

(Milbank, 1990, 245). Milbank critiques liberation theologians for thinking they have moved beyond Catholic social teaching through their analysis of social realities via the social sciences. In reality, he argues, liberation theologians perpetuate belief in a kind of "economic providence" as a "purely immanent process" much like Adam Smith's stoic doctrine of unintended consequences. In such a providential reading of social realities, liberation need not be mediated through a particular set of historical events; it can be found already immanent in the social forces working in history without ecclesial mediation. Milbank critiques Catholic social teaching for being too indebted to a "modern natural law framework," and liberation theology does not escape that framework either. In Milbank's account, the social sciences represent a modern version of the idea of a natural law solely by a doctrine of pure nature.

The Catholic philosopher, Alasdair MacIntyre, also argues that Christianity requires capitalism's abolition, but not on the same theological grounds as Milbank. MacIntyre finds grounds in Catholic social teaching for a moral philosophy, rooted in biblical teaching that refuses "coercive imposition by an external authority" (MacIntyre, 1994, 176). Power and manipulation do not trump truth and goodness. Catholic social teaching (at least as articulated in *Veritatis Splendor*) turns human nature toward the good through a grace that always corrects, completes, and perfects that nature. Such turning toward the good requires "exceptionless negative precepts of the natural law." Without such rules, human nature cannot be turned toward the fullness of goodness; in fact, the "erosion of such rules . . . surrenders human relationship to competing interests and political interests" (MacIntyre, 1994, 185). Modern philosophical notions that reject such teaching have produced "distorted conceptions of freedom" and have turned all "practical situations" into "cost/benefit analyses." Errors in moral teaching—the rejection of rules, a distorted notion of freedom, and the reduction of all relationships to manipulative exchanges of power—produce deformities in political and economic life.

Law directs human action to virtuous ends. Without virtuous ends, law becomes arbitrary and manipulative. MacIntyre finds capitalism to be a consequence of the loss of ends. Thus, because of the logic of the theological virtues, MacIntyre calls Christians to work for capitalism's abolition. Reflecting in 1995 on his 1953 publication, *Marxism and Christianity,* he states:

> What, on a Christian understanding of human and social relationships, does God require of us in those relationships? That we love our neighbours and that we recognize that charity towards them goes beyond, but always includes justice. An adequate regard for justice always involves not only a concern that justice be done and injustice prevented or remedied on any particular occasion, but also resistance to and, where possible, the abolition of institutions that systematically generate injustice. (vii)

One such institution MacIntyre identifies is "the systematic injustices generated by nascent and developed commercial and industrial capitalism" (vii). These injustices are both individual and systemic. They are individual, because capitalism rewards not virtue but vice, allowing vicious persons to benefit at the expense of virtue itself; they are systemic, because at the origin of all accumulation in capitalism are "gross inequalities in the initial appropriation of capital." Capitalism also pits workers against owners, and it refuses to acknowledge legitimate moral teachings on just wages and just prices (ix–x).

In sum, Gutiérrez's opposition to capitalism rests on a social-scientific analysis of reality. Milbank anathematizes capitalist exchanges because of the heretical positions that gave rise to them and which they perpetuate. MacIntyre opposes capitalism because of its historical performance when measured against the norms of faithful practice. Drawing upon orthodox Christian teaching and practice and, in the case of MacIntyre at least, Catholic social teaching, two influential theologians, and one philosopher find capitalism to be sinful at best and heretical at worst. This does not illegitimize the necessary exchanges of the modern corporation, but it means that workers and owners must recognize the heretical assumptions present in these forms of exchange and look for ways, through the church's teaching, to achieve their true end. The story does not end here, however. Other theologians and philosophers, drawing upon the same teachings and tradition, have come to a starkly different conclusion about capitalism.

THE SINFULNESS OF THE SOCIALIST VISION

Some theologians who themselves formerly adhered to a socialist vision now urge theologians to recognize their errors in advocating this vision. Two such theologians are Max Stackhouse and Dennis McCann, who state, "The Protestant Social Gospel, early Christian realism, much neo-orthodoxy, many forms of Catholic modernism, the modern ecumenical drive for racial and social inclusiveness, and contemporary liberation theories all held that democracy, human rights and socialism were the marks of the coming kingdom. For all their prophetic witness in many areas, they were wrong about socialism. The future will not bring what contemporary theology said it would and should" (Stackhouse and McCann, 1995, 949–50). Stackhouse and McCann not only suggest that theologians' commitment to a socialist vision was based on erroneous social analyses; they also charge that commitment with being downright sinful. They write, "The failure of the socialist vision . . . demands repentance." Why? It falsely portrayed capitalism as "greedy, individualistic, exploitative and failing," and socialism as "generous, community-affirming, equitable." Beginning with this false characterization, theologians naïvely taught that the inevitable transition from the former to the latter was what God was "doing in the world." They were wrong.

Inasmuch as Stackhouse and McCann recognize the false immanent economic providence that Protestant and Catholic liberation theology adopted, they are surely correct to call us to repentance. So why should this settle the issue of socialism or capitalism? McCann and Stackhouse's central argument seems to be that socialism's historical performance has inevitably led to "class consciousness," "revolutionary cadres," and "bureaucratized control mechanisms" whereas, capitalism has historically been grounded in the "context-transcending principles of truth, justice, and love," which "protect the moral and spiritual rights of persons and groups and disclose purposes for living that are not of this world" (Stackhouse and McCann, 1995, 950). Theology "shapes social destiny" by offering a vision that protects the individual and the universal, the personal and the cosmopolitan, the material and the spiritual. Christian theology contributes to economic life a universal or cosmopolitan social ethics in which voluntary associations can form the basis for social exchanges based on these "context-transcending principles."

McCann and Stackhouse do not defend a "libertarian neoconservative" capitalism. Instead, they call for a "reformed capitalism," which is one that concedes the propriety of the "profit motive" while calling for restraint. "Creating wealth is the whole point of economic activity," they argue, but the profit motive must be pursued only through "honorable means" (Stackhouse and McCann, 1995, 952). Thus, even these defenders of capitalism recognize it cannot stand as is; it needs reform. McCann and Stackhouse do not draw extensively on Catholic social teaching to make their case against socialism or for a reformed capitalism. However, they could do so, in so far as it is true that Catholic social teaching embodies precisely what Milbank critiques: a form of natural law teaching that does not interject any confessional particularity into a cosmopolitan social ethic.

Michael Novak has defended capitalism against its theological detractors (particularly on the Catholic left) since 1979, when he gave a lecture at the University of Notre Dame on the work of the laity in the world. Like McCann and Stackhouse, Novak's turn toward democratic capitalism entailed a turn away from his former socialist vision. He "welcomed the attempts of the Catholic church to 'modernize' itself," realizing that his former socialism was "formed by a large component of nostalgia for the medieval village" (Novak, 1982, 23–24). Novak does not seem to embrace capitalism as uniquely suitable for Christian or Catholic societies. Many different ethics and cultures can feed it and are compatible with it. Nevertheless, Novak does argue that Christianity created capitalism. Here he agrees with Milbank but, unlike Milbank, he does not see capitalism as the result of distortions in Christian teaching—of heresy. For Novak, capitalism emerges from Christianity because of the latter's rationalization of economic life. Christianity provided the necessary conditions for capitalism because it was congenial to ideas such as "the rule of law and a bureaucracy for resolving disputes rationally; a specialized and mobile labor force; the institutional permanence that allows for transgenerational investment and sustained intellectual and physical efforts, together with the accumulation of long-term capital; and a zest for discovery, enterprise, wealth creation and new undertakings" (Novak, 1999). Novak's defense of capitalism seeks to both draw on and correct Weber's thesis that the rationalization of economic life developed in Protestant cities through the Protestant notion of vocation.[39] Novak locates the origin of capitalism in the Catholic monasteries and rural areas of the Middle Ages. Thus, Novak's argument is much more sociological than theological. Unlike Milbank, he does not first position these developments within a heretical or orthodox reading of the Christian tradition. They are presented, rather, as social facts that are then given theological evaluation. For Novak, the church's role in the creation of capitalism can primarily be defined in sociological terms. What is significant is the administration of the church's holdings through certain bureaucratic structures administered by an entrepreneurial, celibate priesthood, which for Novak was the first "highly motivated, literate, specialized, and mobile labor force."

Novak diverges from other sociological accounts in that he offers theological reasons for why these purely sociological developments were not aberrations from, but rather faithful developments of, Christian doctrine: "Just as Jacques Maritain had recognized in American political institutions the yeast of the Gospels working in history, so also Max Weber had dimly seen that the original impulses of capitalism spring from Christianity, too" (Novak, 1999, 21–29). What Weber saw dimly was the relationship between Christianity and capitalism; what he failed to see was how this relationship could not be accounted for in sociological terms alone. Theological terms are also necessary because, according to Novak, capitalism has an "incarnational" dimension. Novak sets his incarnational theology against an eschatological one. The latter is represented by persons like Dorothy Day and positions itself against the world, whereas the former understands the goodness of the created order.

What does it mean to have an incarnational view of political economy? As Novak explains it,

It is important that there be Christians who go out into this city (the earthly city), whatever its stage of moral and religious development, and try to incarnate the Gospels in it as Jesus incarnated God in history. . . . In my earlier years, I thought the best model for this reconstruction lay in a blend of democracy with some form of socialism. Later, I came to believe that socialism in any of its forms would be futile and destructive. I saw greater hope in a more realistic effort to reform and reconstruct society through the unique combination of capitalism and democracy that we have been lucky enough to inherit in America. But my point is that my own strategic vision, which is incarnational rather than eschatological, has been constant throughout my life. (Novak, 1999, A.18)

The incarnational notion of the corporation can perhaps best be seen in Novak's essay, "Toward a Theology of the Corporation." Here, he notes "when we speak of the body of Christ, we ordinarily mean the Church," but the term *incarnation* can also be properly applied to "the modern business corporation." Exactly what he means here is difficult to assess. I'm sure this likeness is intended metaphorically, similar to the way ecofeminists refer to the earth as "God's body." Both Novak and the ecofeminists draw on a conception of "incarnational" theology that expands the incarnation beyond the threefold form of the body of Christ—the historical body of Jesus, the Sacrament, and the church. However, just as I find the claim of ecofeminism to be such a strange use of theological language that I do not know how to make sense of it, I likewise find the term "incarnation" used with reference to the business corporation so odd that I am not sure how it is to be received in theology. If I have read him correctly, Novak seems to be expanding the traditional notion of Christ's threefold body to include a fourth "incarnation"—the modern business corporation.

### The Theological Difference

What difference does theology make for how we can speak well of God and the modern corporation? Novak would seem to find both the shrimp and lobster plant as well as the water meter corporation to be an incarnation of God's presence. However, in presenting a fourth form of the body of Christ, and without explaining how it is related to the other three forms, his work loses the capacity to speak well about God and, thus, cannot speak well about the corporation either.

McCann and Stackhouse's notion of the modern corporation as a potential "worldly ecclesia" is less objectionable than Novak's. But neither do they explain to us how this worldly ecclesia and the ecclesia itself relate. In fact, their desire to avoid confessional particularity in theology in favor of a cosmopolitan social ethic leads them to lose any sense of both the particularity of the church and the locality of the corporation. The global nature of the corporation requires it to break through cultural and social boundaries and set up universal forms of community beyond biological, cultural, and social ties. This is why the corporation is a worldly ecclesia. Indeed, one sign of the goodness of the modern corporation is that it "has found a home in societies far from its roots." In fact, McCann and Stackhouse go so far as to argue, "Businesses increasingly operate in a context of global competition. Comparative advantage can make selling out, closing down or moving to other lands imperative. The failure to move is in some cases a manifestation of a misplaced patriotism, and may fail to aid underdeveloped regions" (Stackhouse and McCann, 1995, 952). They do note that the pressure to move is a temptation that could be resisted. But in their way of thinking a commitment to locale and place can also be a refusal to engage in the missionary work that the Christian doctrine of vocation entails—a work that the corporation, as a social body—is also called to carry out.[40]

For Stackhouse and McCann, the modern corporation, as a "worldly ecclesia," is a "secular form of covenantal community." It has a legitimate, if limited, function. However, they do not portray the corporation as an incarnation of Christ, as does Novak. Novak is clear that when he speaks of the corporation as incarnating Christ he intends precisely "the multinational corporation" that "build[s] manufacturing or other facilities in other lands in order to operate there." He speaks of the "grace" in these corporations and refers to these multinational corporations as not only "incarnational" but also "sacramental." Novak's terminology does not help us understand the theological significance of either of our corporations, but merely functions as a legitimating discourse that prevents the proper theological task of discerning faithful and faithless forms of exchange. Novak offers impoverished dogma.

Milbank helps us describe the corrupt practices of the shrimp and lobster plant as a violation of the charitable exchange that is a Christian ontology. This ontology can only be known through the historically contingent mediation of the church, but that does not limit its political and social implications to the church alone for it remains an ontology, even if it lacks a foundation outside historical mediation. And what other kind of ontology is there? As I hope to show, capitalism itself assumes a different kind of ontology, historically mediated by a stoic theology.

MacIntyre helps us name the corrupt practices of the lobster plant as a violation of the virtue of justice and, thus, a violation of Catholic social teaching on the just wage. Both Milbank and MacIntyre might have more difficulty in identifying the virtue present in the midwestern corporation; for it, too, occurs only within systems of capitalist exchange they both find uncharitable and unjust. How might they account for the genuine goodness of this corporation, given the heretical status they attribute to capitalist forms of exchange? Perhaps they could argue that, given the ontological claims the historical practices of Christianity entail, we should not be surprised that cooperation is more basic than competitiveness even in a corporation operating within a capitalist context. Peace and harmony are more basic to our being than vice, violence, and competitiveness. Catholic social teaching reminds us of this fact, even if it does not provide any guarantee that embodying the ontological priority of peace will ensure higher profits. Like the church's teachings on biological reproduction and just war, its assumptions about harmonious cooperation and just wages are to be embodied because they bear witness to God's good creation, not because they "work" in a world still characterized, even at the end of history, by rebellion against God. Both Milbank and MacIntyre seem to suggest that some remediation for injustice can be found by conceding to workers' just wages, which would include some ownership in the very corporation their labor makes possible; they maintain a socialist vision—although neither would present that socialist version in Marxist terms or accept uncritically the labor theory of value. In fact, they both recognize that capitalist exchanges assume and require liberalism's cultural assumptions, particularly about the individual and the separation into separate spheres of religion, politics, and economics.[41]

Rather than assuming the legitimacy of a cosmopolitan social ethic, Milbank and MacIntyre teach us to view critically the history within which the modern corporation has emerged. This history makes possible value in exchange more so than any labor, consumer, or exchange theory of value. And this history repeats theological affirmations, particularly an immanent providential theology, which naturally emerges in theologies that seek to be relevant to the modern corporation precisely because the history within which these forms of exchange arose assumes that same Stoic immanent providential theology. It will appear natural only when we refuse to historicize its own development. By explaining how capitalism assumes a confessional theology just as much as does Christian dogma and Catholic social teaching, I hope to show why the arguments present in theologians such as Gutiérrez, Stackhouse, McCann, and Novak do not work.

### Stoic Theology or Catholic Social Teaching

I have suggested that no definitive account of the "real" exists apart from a particular historical language. This may seem to be, for some, a trivial truism or, for others, too much a concession to skepticism, but that is not my intention. Instead, what I hope to show is that any social analysis of the reality of the lobster and watermeter plants will always and already come to us through language such that no easy distinction is possible between a sphere ruled by a natural causality explainable by natural laws and another sphere ruled by freedom and in which morality and theology prevail.[42]

Two dominant theological languages seek to render intelligible the kind of economic exchanges found in the lobster and watermeter corporations.[43] Inasmuch as the corrupt practices of the former are read as a "social fact" that is necessary within a progressive development (either within capitalism itself or from mercantilism to capitalism, or even as a stage in the transition from capitalism to socialism), then the theological language that makes such a social fact appear will be Adam Smith's stoic theology. However, if one sees these exchanges under the aspect of the language of Catholic social teaching, a radically different social fact emerges.

Smith's stoic theology helps us understand why some persons justify the sacrifices Guarifuna men and women make for the sake of others' fast-food consumption. It assumes his "doctrine of unintended consequences." When Smith argues that "by pursuing his own interests" an individual "frequently promotes that of the society more effectually than when he really intends to promote it," he drew on his earlier notion of a stoic doctrine of providence (Smith, 1965, 423). To argue that the unjust situation of the shrimp and lobster plant is a necessary social fact contributing to the future development of the Guarifuna people is, thus, to accept Smith's stoic theology. It is to accept the idea that there is an economic providence intrinsic to social reality whereby sacrifices are required by some for the sake of a future development that will justify those sacrifices. This idea makes capitalism both a kind of theodicy and eschatology. It is not theologically neutral.

Smith's implicit theology cannot be an option for Christian theologians, especially for those operating within the tradition of Catholic social teaching with its longstanding commitment to the just wage and the concept of intrinsic evils. This is to say that some actions can never be undertaken, even on the assumption of a greater future benefit, because such actions cannot be turned toward God, who is humanity's chief end. This teaching only makes sense if, as John Paul II has stated, we need not assume a tragic world in which every good done to someone entails an evil done to someone else. The exceptionless moral norm, of which the just wage teaching is an example, only makes sense against the backdrop of a Christian theology in which our lives are to be obedient to Christ. We can take the risk of obedience and not simply think of all actions in terms of cost/benefit ratios because Christ has shown us what a true and good performance of humanity is. We understand creation, incarnation, and the "natural" only by examining

Christ's life. Any theology that plays one of these themes against another part of the Christian story—that proceeds as if the incarnation can be discussed without also discussing the Crucifixion and eschatology, or as if creation can be understood without Christology—vivisects the body of Christ.

If reading social reality through Smith's stoic theology is a necessary feature of capitalist exchanges, as I think it is, then should Christians pursue a socialist vision? Is it proper to see the relationship between owners, managers, shareholders, and workers as a clash of interests only to be remedied when workers own the means of production (for what else could we mean by socialism)? This, too, seems to conflict with Catholic social teaching; for it continually presents social reality not as fundamentally antagonistic, but as ontologically peaceable. If socialism assumes that all that binds us together is power, then like capitalism, it must be rejected. Manipulative power-relations may be the social bonds we have inherited, but—if Catholic social teaching is correct—the clash of interests such relations represent is not intrinsic to social reality. It is, rather, a sign of rebellion against God's goodness, a sign that, oddly enough, results from a historical tradition that presents itself as a putatively neutral, objective, rational, and ahistorical social analysis. This very analysis requires the positing of a "social fact" in which social relationships are reduced to power—both in theory and in practice—so that they can then be regulated.

Rejecting the reduction of all social relations to manipulative power exchanges is part of reconstituting new social practices. For theory and practice, like fact and value or nature and freedom, do not constitute autonomous realms. The reason I think Christianity must continue to be open to socialism in a way that it cannot be open toward capitalism is not because of socialism's historical performance. McCann and Stackhouse are correct to call us to repent of any kind of "scientific socialism" that seeks to rationalize struggle and antagonism through an immanent providential theology. The very fact that a corporation like the midwestern plant can survive within capitalism demonstrates other possibilities for work that need not assume a stoic natural theology in which vice more than virtue contributes to the common good, and in which a fundamental antagonism rules us all. If socialism holds forth the possibility that workers can share ownership in their labor in a non-competitive system in which the interests of owners, shareholders, and workers need not—by some necessity of a natural social fact—be pitted against each other, then yes, Christianity must continue to hold forth the possibility of socialism and work for the abolition of capitalism.

# — 8 —

## OFFERING OUR GIFTS

## The Politics of Remembrance

How should we read economic exchanges? For Christian theology they must be read in terms of the offering we present to Christ in our worship. This is the work that fulfills our purpose as creatures. The central act of this worship is the Holy Eucharist. It compels us to ask how the gifts we exchange there illumine the necessary economic exchanges in our every day life. Can they generate the social bonds that render those exchanges intelligible? These questions seem odd to those of us who received our education in the modern university; for the university divides disciplines such as theology, politics, and economics into distinct autonomous fields of study—assuming each can give an account of itself without the need for the other. Politics and economics explain the facts of social bonds; their subject matter is the distribution of power and analysis of exchange.

Whatever modern theology does, it does not seem to do that. It sets forth values or answers questions of meaning. It only indirectly relates to politics and economics. Yet, it was not always so. Eamon Duffy explains how Sunday ceremonies of the Eucharistic celebration in sixteenth-century England were essential to social arrangements and the distribution of power. They both "promoted harmony" and "imposed hegemony." Where laity stood in the processional, who kissed the paxbread first, and who provided the Eucharistic bread for the celebration were all matters that produced social harmony as well as division.

In some places the bread itself was cut into varying sizes dependent upon one's social rank. In 1518, John "Kareless" was accused of the deadly vice of pride for "taking too large a piece of the holy loaf." Not only the reception of the Holy Loaf, but also the gifts that persons offered to the church for the celebration of the Mass were causes for social harmony as well as hegemony. They were how persons would be remembered at the great moment of the Eucharistic celebration. As Duffy notes, "again and again one encounters bequests of linen for use in the Mass. Gifts of this sort gave those of modest means a way of perpetuating their personal presence at the heart of the community" (Duffy, 1992, 126–28). The "gift" of the Eucharist and the gifts church people brought to it—for better or worse—established social bonds. The politics and economics of a sixteenth-century English village were inseparable from theological concerns.

We do not live in sixteenth-century England. Neither the Eucharist nor the church gives our everyday social life its political or economic orientation. Yet, even to have an orientation is to be residually affected by that other world, for it is to be directed toward some end. As Albert Borgmann notes, the term *orientation* arose from the way cathedrals once shaped daily life. They were built toward the east, bearing witness to where Christian hope was directed—toward the homeland of Christ, who would one day return. They structured the time and space of everyday life seeking to orient us by the virtues of hope and faith toward our true end, which was to be found in Christ (Borgmann, 1987, 72). Most people still seem to have some orientation to their lives; we are not simply spinning on a little blue ball ride through a vast nothingness "plunging continually, backward, sideward, forward, in all directions" (Nietzsche, 1983, 95). While the space and time of modern life are not so structured as to orient us to the end of Christ, our lives are routinely oriented. They are oriented by "interstate highways" that give access to malls and other major business attractions. The patterns and practices of our lives orient us in the world first and foremost as consumers. We are all consumers whose end is to buy and sell within the market place—"24/7." This is the default position of our orientation much as the orientation provided by the Eucharist was the default position in sixteenth-century England. If our lives can still be oriented by the gift of the Eucharist, it will require a particular intentionality and attentiveness on our part.

What difference would it make to have our lives, especially the everyday exchanges that provide our daily sustenance, more oriented by the gifts one finds in the church's liturgy than by the interstate highways that give us our direction? This chapter will address that question, working with the assumption that such an ecclesial orientation is still present—even if only residually so—in the church's liturgical life. We do not need to invent something new to produce this other orientation. We do not even need some cataclysmic revolution. Instead, we need to be attentive to what God already gives us and learn to recognize the competing practices that orient our lives in directions other than that of this gift. In fact, we will argue, the distinguishing practices between lives oriented by the gift found in the church's liturgy and one found on the interstate highways is the difference between *gift* and *contract*.

### Bringing Our Gifts to the Altar

After sharing the peace and before praying the Great Thanksgiving, Christians are instructed to bring an offering to the altar. This practice occurs among diverse churches and usually includes tokens of people's everyday livelihood. For instance, in Wesleyan Churches in Haiti, this offering includes the basic produce of everyday life; vegetables, chickens, hogs, and even donkeys are brought to the altar. Worship proceeds amid the chaos of fluttering wings and braying beasts as all these gifts are received before the congregation shares together in the Lord's Supper. In most mainline churches, the offering is more civil. It is usually a collection of money brought forward with the elements—the bread and wine—to be used for the Eucharistic celebration. Yet, what are the gifts we offer at the altar? What is their purpose? Few persons would be so crass as to think that the tokens we bring are presented to buy God's favor. They are not akin to economic transactions where an exchange occurs for the sake of goods or services rendered. Why then bring any gift at all?

The gift we bring only makes sense when it is brought along with the bread and wine that will represent Christ's body for us. The gift that the Christian church offers at the altar is not the produce of our own labor, it is instead the gift of Christ's offering for us. It is this gift that we offer to God. It is why in the United Methodist Church we pray, "in remembrance of these your mighty acts in Jesus Christ, we offer ourselves in praise and thanksgiving as a holy and living sacrifice, in union with Christ's offering for us. . . ." Similarly, the Great Thanksgiving in the Anglican *Book of Common Prayer* states, "We celebrate the memorial of our redemption, O Father, in this sacrifice of praise and thanksgiving. Recalling his death, resurrection, and ascension, we offer you these gifts." What are "these gifts"? They are the elements, which will be for us the body and blood of Christ as we remember his deeds on our behalf. In other words, the gift that we offer to God is first and foremost the gift God himself has given to us. We offer him the gift of the Son's sacrifice for our sins; this gift renders intelligible all the other gifts we bring, including all the physical and intellectual gifts that we have and are—the bodily labor that sustains our daily life, as well as our capacities for speech and thought that issue forth in praise and thanksgiving. Our hope is that everything in our daily lives will now participate in Christ's obedience. For those of us who hope to find our orientation through Christian worship, this gift should provide it.

## Is Such a Gift Possible?

What should be less controversial than the goodness of a gift, which allows us to see all our lives within the context of God's gift to us? Although what is good has been, is, and probably always will be contested, a gift might be considered an unproblematic good. The very language of "gift economy" sounds preferable to an economy based on "contract." Would we not rather see our lives in relation to others in terms of gifts than contracts? To invoke the term, gift is to rally persons around something seemingly good. But is such a gift possible? Or is it a subtle and, therefore, dangerous form of manipulation, especially when that gift is proclaimed as God's own self? Is it social harmony that this gift seeks to provide for us, or is it social hegemony?

None of us asked Christ to give himself to redeem us from our sins. Such a gift happened to us, before we were born. We incur guilt because our forbearers and we sinned, but God chooses not to impute this guilt to us. Instead, God forgives us our sin if we receive the gift Christ offers. Those who refuse the gift risk losing eternal blessedness for the hell of life without God. Such inequality seems beyond manipulative; it can easily appear tyrannical. Each person is eternally responsible for his or her reception or refusal of a gift for which he or she did not ask. As John Leonard has noted, this kind of inequality is precisely why the portrayal of Satan in Milton's *Paradise Lost* is so seductive. Satan refuses to be manipulated by the gift and rallies over one-third of the angels to make the same refusal through a stirring proclamation of liberty and equality:

> Will ye submit your necks, and
> Choose to bend
> The supple knee? Ye will not, if

> I trust
> To know ye right, or if ye know
> Yourselves
> Natives and sons of Heav'n
> Possessed before
> By none, and if not equal all, yet
> Free
> Equally free.
> > (Milton in Leonard, 2002, 28)

Does not the reception of this gift force us into a burdensome situation of an eternally bended knee, constantly expressing our gratitude for a gift for which we did not ask? What could be more manipulative, hegemonic, and ultimately oppressive than this? We are eternally indebted for a gift we did not seek.

Perhaps gift should not be so easily celebrated, not only when it comes to God's gift of the Son poured out for us, but also when gift is asserted as the basis for political and social bonds. Gift economies can easily imply gross inequalities and burdensome obligations we can never forget. In a gift economy, there is no clear measure by which one can know that debts have been discharged. There is never a point at which the debt can simply be forgotten. The memory of the debt requires reciprocal gifts that never come to an end. The bonds of obligation remain in perpetuity.

Some anthropologists argue that pre-modern cultures were bound together by such a gift-exchange economy. In his book *The Gift: The Form and Reason for Exchange in Archaic Societies*, anthropologist Marcel Mauss argues that the root of all economic exchange lies not in bartering, but in gift giving. In a gift-giving community, persons are engaged in perpetual exchanges that bind one to another for the common good. To give a gift is to request that a gift be given in return; to accept a gift is to commit oneself to such an economy. In a culture constituted by this kind of politics, everything is based on reciprocity. The gift-giving community is a social and political community that subsumes all dimensions of life. It is what Mauss calls the "potlatch"—the place of being satiated. The potlatch is the system of total services in which the legal, economic, political, religious, and moral can only be harmonized by the activity of gift giving (Mauss, 1990, 5–7).

Though this economy appears to be premised upon a notion of voluntarism, it is actually an obligatory form of participation. There are no such things as free or pure gifts; there is only gift-exchange. As all are required to be donors, all are also required to be recipients. To refuse reciprocation places the act of giving outside of any mutual ties; it relinquishes any future claims one may have on another. Donors who imagine themselves exempt from reception deny the telos of such an economy. Likewise, to refuse to receive is to refuse to give. Such non-participation is tantamount to declaring war as it rejects the bonds of commonality. It denies that the future recipient maintains any claims over the goods in question and obliterates the common relationship needed in order to sustain a gift economy (Mauss, 1990, 13). Nothing can be held in perpetuity and no one is ever exempted for the ongoing process of recycling gifts. For this reason, the gift economy is a more visible economy than the free-market economy of late modernity. In the former, everything is for passing on; goods are a good because they are never alienated from the common life.

This kind of gift giving may still be present in modern economic arrangements. In his *Sex and Love in the Home*, David McCarthy presents an economy based on "neighborly gift-exchange," which "has its foundation within the temporal structure of common life and the ad hoc currency of the non-identical gift" (McCarthy, 2001, 105). Daily exchanges such as watching each other's children, providing meals, and shoveling snow are not done in terms of the contractual exchanges of identical gifts that take place in malls, fast food restaurants, and banks. Yet, as McCarthy points out, gift-exchanges are not without expectations. They bind us together through obligations, which are risky precisely because they are "non-identical." We are not certain where the obligation begins or ends.

Stock options and signing bonuses may be simulacra of a "neighborly gift-exchange." They, too, are nonidentical exchanges that go beyond a bare exchange of identical proportions. A CEO who is given stock options is given a gift of a future possibility that ties his or her gift to the performance of the stock (not necessarily to the good of the corporation and, thus, it is a simulacra of a neighborly gift-exchange). If the stock increases substantially, the CEO is able to purchase the stock at the contracted price when he or she signed on as chief administrator. The difference between the stock's increase in value and the stock price at signing seems to be a gift beyond the strict requirements of payment for services rendered. But has not this kind of gift exchange destroyed lives and corporations? Are not gifts inherently manipulative? Are they not merely concealed forms of privilege and power? Given the problematic nature of gifts, it comes as no surprise that in modern political arrangements where liberty and equality rule—like Satan in Paradise Lost—gifts are rendered apolitical. Instead of any gift economy, a strict notion of equality measured by contract seeks to define all our exchanges and, thus, orient our lives.

### LIBERAL REDEMPTION: CONTRACT AND FORGETTING

Within the tradition of liberalism, social bonds are to be regulated by contracts so that we will know when our obligation begins and ends. Once the contract rules us, we are not bound to the giver beyond that to which we willingly consent. When I purchase produce at the local supermarket, the only exchange presented to me depends upon the value of the produce before me. Once I have paid the requisite amount, no other obligation remains. I do not need to know how the vegetables I purchase were grown, harvested, and shipped. I am under no obligation to determine whether the price I paid can sustain the lives of those who make my consumption possible. I need to know one thing—what is the value of this product? If I find my agent-satisfaction increased by parting with my money in order to consume this product, then I will rationally choose to do so until it no longer benefits my agent-satisfaction. This form of rationality, known as "marginal utility," becomes the only form of rationality I need in order to engage in reasonable economic exchanges. I am an individual in the market place who has no other obligations than those that I choose, and I choose them solely based on whether or not I consent to the value of the product presented to me.

The exchange that occurs in the market place assumes liberal political society with its originating myth where, in order to secure my individual will from onslaught by unnecessary burdens, each individual gives the trust of her or his individual will to the sovereign authority, who then preserves us as individuals against each other. We primarily need protection from each other and this protection provides the bonds of society. The capitalist market is an extension of this notion of liberal political society. Each individual meets in the market place in order to buy and sell based solely on his or her individual freedom to do so. As long as these exchanges do not fundamentally call into question the conditions of liberal society itself, they can be pursued. The notion of "contract" ensures that the exchange is consensual, based on the individual's will. Whether the exchange is for food, clothing, sexual intercourse, a mortgage, or education, an explicit or implicit contract defines the terms of the agreement such that the expectations of fulfillment are clear and as precise as possible. We are all individual consumers engaging in mutually consensual transactions.

John Stuart Mill recognized that the political and social basis for the orienting power of individual consumption was "liberty." For Mill, individuals must be free to enter into any exchange they deem conducive to their own interest, including even exchanges of "fornication" and "gambling," which require the toleration of "pimping" and "keeping a gambling house." The only qualification to this liberty is that persons should not be coerced. They enter into exchanges "either wisely or foolishly, on their own prompting, as free as possible from the arts of persons who stimulate their inclinations for interested purposes of their own" (Mill, 1975, 97). But each individual must be made free from any undue obligation imposed by another. Under such conditions one can then enter into any exchange one desires for it will be freely entered into. Contracts are means by which such freely entered agreements can be protected and achieved.

This could potentially prevent the kind of abusive gift exchanges noted previously. Contracts are an attempt to insure consensual exchanges. When I enter into an exchange with a mortgage company, we have clear expectations of each other. They tell me how many payments I must give them, when I must make the payments, and what the penalties will be if I am late. We are both clear when our relationship will come to an end. In fact, when that relationship comes to an end we no longer have reason to be in contact with each other. We can forget each other. I do not expect them to relate to me as in a gift economy. They do not give me money and say, "Here is the money, pay it back when you get the chance. If we need something from you, we will let you know." That would make us both nervous. How could they be certain I will not refuse to fulfill my debts to them without penalty? How could I be certain that what they need from me will be appropriate and will come at an appropriate time? If we do not have clear contractual obligations, then any gift economy will make us more dependent upon each other. Contracts are intended to protect us from such dependence. They provide the necessary distance from each other that prevents undue obligations.

### GIFTS: OUTSIDE POLITICS

Contracts seek to insure that all our exchanges are consensual, based on the freedom of the individual will to consent. They free us from the possibility of burdensome obligations a gift economy imposes.

However, once contract defines economic and political bonds, gift-exchange no longer has a political role. Gift is rendered apolitical, outside the city where, as Aristotle noted, only a god or a beast can survive. It comes as no surprise that within liberal political and economic systems where social bonds are based upon clearly defined and precisely calculated exchanges, the notion of "gift" becomes defined as disinterested and unconditional. A gift does not function like McCarthy's "neighborly gift exchange." Instead, a gift becomes that which is given without any expectation of return. Gift cannot orient our lives; it no longer has that kind of political power. Not even God's own gift can accomplish a political orientation once we are all individuals, bound by contracts of our own choosing that free us from each other. Contractual exchanges allow us to forget everything but whether or not we were free when we chose this rather than that. It is not surprising that Christology—especially Christ's resurrection from the dead—becomes problematic under such social conditions.

In an effort to avoid any hint of a contract, Christian ethics depoliticized the notion of gift, particularly through modern interpretations of Christian love as disinterested. For instance, Anders Nygren defines the essence of Christian love, which he terms agape, as a gift given without any thought of return. It is completely disinterested. In similar fashion, Søren Kierkegaard argues that the apex of Christian love is found in loving the dead because in loving the dead the lover's love cannot be reciprocated—it is purely selfless (Kierkegaard , 1995, 345–59). This agapic form of love from both Nygren and Kierkegaard influenced the work of many twentieth-century Christians, including the prominent Christian ethicist Reinhold Niebuhr. In Niebuhr, Christian ethics becomes self-sacrificial. My action is only truly loving when I do it solely with regard to someone else's benefit and not to my own. It must be "disinterested." For this reason, the truly loving action becomes characterized by crucifixion and death. The resurrection, especially the resurrection of the body, is rendered problematic. For it still smacks of a return. But of course, such loving actions are always a-political; they take place "outside the city" where only fools and martyrs reside. They are to be applauded and celebrated, but they are apolitical.

If gift is rendered apolitical in modern society, might it return in a postmodern era? Insofar as postmodernity remains inevitably linked with the modern, we should expect that here, too, gift is, at best, a renunciation of all temporal political and social bonds for the sake of a superhuman act of unconditional sacrifice, one that can only finally assume death as its end. For only when my gift ends in my own death can I truly know that I did not reduce gift to a contract. Only then can I be certain that the gift is given "without strings," such that I truly did not expect return. It is no surprise then, that given the tight link between modernity and postmodernity, death becomes the greatest of all gifts—the only way to escape the temporal order and its inevitable generalities. This can be seen in Jacques Derrida's work where he writes, "The absoluteness of duty and responsibility presume that one denounce, refute and transcend at the same time, all duty, all responsibility, and every human law. It calls for a betrayal of everything that manifests itself within the order of universal generality . . ." (Derrida, 1995, 66). Ethics assumes a singularity, an unconditioned givenness, that refuses everything that has come before, everything that has been measured, ruled, generalized into a law or tradition. Heresy becomes dogma. Everything else must be deconstructed for the sake of the unconditioned call to act in the moment with no expectation of return. Only such an act can truly account for a gift.

Surely, "contract" is safer than "gift." It preserves our independence and equality. It prevents us from "bending the supple knee" before those who would seek our indebtedness, whether it be temporal or eternal powers who do so. Contract is a hedge against hegemony. The modern notion of contract seems preferable to the notion of gift. But has the reduction of exchanges to contractual-consensual relations given us the promised freedom? Are we yet "possessed by none" but ourselves, each equally free from the other? In fact, the opposite occurred in the modern era. The more we seek to be free from the other by social bonds determined by identical exchanges, the more these bonds take over our lives and force us into a single common orientation; we are all required to be individuals whose reasonableness depends on our will to consume. This increasingly defines every social relation—family, marriage, neighborhoods, friendships, university, and the church. This squeezes out any possibility of seeing our lives and work as gift. Gifts provide no political orientation. The social bonds I inhabit are simply those of my own choosing—they are all "limited liability" relationships with clear and nameable endpoints, along with escape clauses to help me end them when my will so chooses.

## A DIFFERENT KIND OF GIFT: THE POLITICS OF REMEMBERING

Perhaps we think of gift, including the gift of God's own self in the Eucharist, as separate from political and economic matters because our lives become oriented only by the practice of contract that a consumerist culture demands of us than by the liturgical offering present in the Eucharist. Contracts, of course, are not evil in themselves. But they cannot provide the social bonds for a true, good, and just politics. Once contract alone defines social bonds then Christ's gift becomes a problem precisely because I did not consent to it. Such a gift need not even be refused for it has no necessary hold on my will in the first place, unless I first give it such a hold. Even then, I can tacitly recognize that any hold it has will be conditioned by my own choosing and not because I am somehow necessarily obligated by a gift given before my will even was.

However, when we make this argument we find ourselves in accord with Milton's Satan, and perhaps that should cause us to pause. When we find ourselves trapped in this kind of perverse logic perhaps we have not yet understood the nature of gift (or the nature of God). As John Milbank argues, a genuine gift is neither unconditional nor disinterested. In fact, a genuine gift like erotic love "is most free where it is yet most bound, most mutual and most reciprocally demanded" (Milbank, 1995, 124). Gifts then are not the opposite of contracts. Like contracts, they assume a return; but unlike contracts, the return never ends. My reception of a gift from another and the consequent return leads us more fully into the life of the other while also fulfilling my own life. For this reason, a gift economy is a virtuous economy. As Alasdair MacIntyre notes, virtues are not grounded in competitive practices where one person's excellence can only be had at the expense of another, but virtue implies a "cooperative social practice" where one person's achieving or fulfilling her proper function helps the other fulfill her excellence as well (MacIntyre, 1984, 187).

The virtues here are not simply means between a deficiency and excess. They are plenteous such that they can never be exhausted. The infused virtues of faith, hope, and love are inexhaustible, because they are the very life of the Holy Spirit who is Gift. Thomas Aquinas argued that the Holy Spirit is properly named Gift. The Spirit is the Gift (*Donum*), who is the Love, proceeding from the Father and Son. The Spirit is also the Gift-given (*Datum*) who makes possible our creation and redemption. Because the Spirit cannot be alienated from the Giver, the Spirit is given without any intention of a return (with no *intentione retributionis*, according to Thomas). It is something that cannot be alienated, and cannot be returned in kind, even though it can be given to another and become his as well (*ST* Ia 38; Aquinas, 1948). Whenever such a gift is received, it becomes conformed to our very being. Thus, we turn to God and offer it in praise and thanksgiving. Such a gift-giving economy draws us closer into the life of God, a life that knows no lack. This is why the Christian doctrines of *creatio ex nihilo* and God's impassibility are so important for a proper understanding of a gift economy.

God did not have to create, nor become bodily present in Jesus. God does not create or redeem to satisfy some lack in God's own nature. It is not a return that satisfies something God does not yet have. God is already the fullness of being, given in God's own self—

through the processions of the Triune Persons. Thomas Weinandy notes that only God can truly be "gift." All human giving is only *partial*, for the person who gives "must do so only through mediating words (words of kindness and love) and actions (hugs, kisses, sexual relations, etc.) which express only a partial giving of oneself even if one's intention is to give the whole of oneself." But the Triune processions are true gifts. "The persons of the Trinity are eternally constituted in their own singular identity only in relation to one another, and thus they subsist as who they are only within their mutual relationships" (Weinandy, 2000, 116). Our gifts are, at best, analogical participations in the Gift, which is "the more excellent way"—the Triune God. God is always already complete, the full actualization of being that needs nothing outside him in order to complete himself.

God is pure act and pure gift. The fact that creation exists bears witness to God's goodness as gift. It is not a contractual relationship where God and creation meet in the market place to bargain over debts. The gift of the Son, like the gift of creation itself, comes to us solely out of God's good abundance. This does not mean it is "unconditional." God gives to us what God is—the goodness of being. We are to participate in that goodness and this is the purpose for our being. We are called to reciprocate the gift of being by participating in its goodness. But this is always a non-identical reciprocation. We cannot create being ex nihilo; we participate in it by reciprocating God's good gifts with God and each other. The Christian recognizes, as fundamental to her narrative, her place as a contingent creature. Such a status reminds us that we exist as gift. Gifts do not end in death or disinterested love; rather, they end in a life returned to God.

Of course, as MacIntyre also reminds us, the cooperative internal goods of virtues only exist within institutional structures where some goods are competitive and therefore scarce. While the virtues of knowledge and wisdom are non-competitive, they are often cultivated in institutional contexts where funding is competitive.

There are inevitable limits we discover even in our pursuit of non-competitive goods. When John "Kareless" takes too much of the holy loaf, less is left for others. Even though we need not capitulate to the basic premise of economists that every good is intrinsically scarce and, thus, the first task of the economist is the efficient distribution of scarce goods, we must nevertheless recognize that limits exist. To learn to live within those limits, even while pursuing limitless goods like God's own goodness, is to become a moral subject (Williams, 2000, 139–54).

## The Gift of Life

For the Christian, the contrast between living into God's life, which is an inexhaustible gift, and the limitations of inevitably sinful structures, means that the truly Christian life could end in martyrdom. This is not self sacrifice and should be distanced from any notion of *agape* as unconditional. In martyrdom, the believer's life is literally returned to God, and this is what makes such a witness possible. But not even in martyrdom do we offer a counter-gift equivalent to the gift of Christ's sacrifice for us. Though martyrdom is, in the words of Tertullian, Origen, and a host of other theologians, a perfecting of the Christian life (martyrdom itself is understood as a gift), the giving of Christ's sacrifice at the altar is the substance of the counter-gift in question. This is not to pit these two liturgical performances against one another—for neither is intelligible without the other. It is rather to say that what is given at the altar is the sacrifice of Jesus, which is not only his death, but even more importantly his resurrected life—a bodily presence that is no longer bound by the limitations of space and time. Death cannot overcome it. Jesus can be fully present in each person's bodily eating of the Eucharist and yet, Jesus will never be exhausted.

Christians, therefore, reside in a constant state of thanksgiving—a perpetual Eucharist. In this ongoing exchange of divine gift and human response is the "living through the offering (*through* the offering, through the *offering*) of the gift given to us of God himself in the flesh." The appropriate response is not one of spontaneous love arising out of one's own volition (as if communion can be sought without God first pursuing us). Rather, the appropriate response is to *"repeat differently*, in order to repeat, *exactly*, the content of Christ's life, and to wait, by a necessary *delay*, the answering repetition of the other that will fold temporal linearity back into the eternal circle of the triune life" (Milbank, 1995, 152; italics in original). By arguing that delay and non-identical repetition constitute a gift-exchange economy, Milbank is suggesting that for a gift to be a gift demands that a gift be given in return. Despite our best self-sacrificial sensibilities, a gift-*exchange* is the only kind of gift truly open to us as creatures. No anonymous relationships between donors and recipients can ultimately prevail. Who we are is determined by the gifts we receive and return—or fail therein.

To give a gift is to engage in a political act. It creates an economy predicated on mutual participation that narrates realities such as "independence" or "self sacrifice" as fictitious. This is not to say that the sacrifices one makes for others are an illusion, rather the sacrifices are only intelligible in light of the social mode of being made possible by communal practices of gift-giving. Such practices do not originate within the will of an individual or a community; instead, they find their basis in that eschatological marriage between God and the church.

### Remembering Our Debts

Being wed to God, of course, is no easy matter. The church seems such an ineffectual and diseased vessel that it is easy to look elsewhere for our orientation—to forget a "Catholic" church in favor of a "global" market. The temptation toward adultery seems, at times, almost overwhelming. Much of our infidelity occurs because we forget to whom we belong as church. There is an ancient Jewish aphorism that says: "Memory is the pillar of redemption; forgetfulness is the beginning of death." In a capitalist-consumer culture, we are habituated in certain economic practices that train us in the art of forgetfulness and invite us to love death (Pickstock, 1998, 101–19). We are ever in search of the "new and improved" that comes to us only as we negate the old and outdated. We buy, we use, and we discard ad infinitum. This is not only the case with automobiles; it also becomes true of theology and Christian practices. The church itself desperately searches for the right niche market to sell its wares, and we are all too willing to forget who we are for the sake of market shares. This is precisely why the repetition of the liturgical performance of the Eucharist and the bringing forth of our own offering can be a radical political act. It causes us to see our everyday lives in terms of the orientation Christ gave and gives us.

In an effort to guard against amnesia, the church performs particular liturgical rituals that function as story-telling devices reminding us who we are and how our lives are to make sense. The Eucharist is *the* reminder par excellence. This act of remembrance makes possible that form of Christ's body known as the church. To say that the Eucharist is an act of remembrance is not to evoke images of a static event, for this memorial is a "living memorial." It reminds "the reminded" that certain practices can only make sense if Jesus has been raised from the dead. If this is true, that is, if Jesus has been raised from the dead, then in the words of Wendell Berry, we, too, must "practice resurrection" (Berry, 1991, 62). If we forget Christ's resurrection, we will not be able to remember well what we ourselves are called to practice.

The gift that is the Eucharist is the gift that obligates its consumers to love one's neighbor as Christ loved us all. Just as Christ refused disobedience even to the point of the cross, so should we; as Christ shared food with one another, so should we; as Christ dispossessed himself, so should we. Those believers who dine on the body of Christ become Christ as they pledge to imitate his love. In so far as believers do this, they make Christ present to the world. As the Mennonite theologian John Rempel argues, in its role as the embodiment of the Church's daily exchanges, the Eucharist is the *sine qua non* of the Church (Rempel, 1993, 88). There can be no understanding of the gift that is the Eucharist that does not in some way shape how Christians are to live in a forgetful world. It renders possible—and necessary—the copious sharing of goods by which all are nourished and sustained. Our material goods generate friendship as the giving away of goods necessitates a reception of goods. Milbank claims that the Eucharist "positions each and every one of us only as fed . . . and bizarrely assimilates us to the food we eat, so that we, in turn, must exhaust ourselves as nourishment for others" (Milbank, 1992, 342). In consuming the flesh and blood of Christ, we participate in the ultimate giving away: the giving away of Christ's body. In this act we become Christ's body, which, once it is in us, cannot be contained but must be shared. It is not conformed to us; but we are conformed to it. To remember this gift as a gift-exchange is to participate in the divine economy whereby Christians are taken into the life of the triune God and become Christ on earth.

Participation in the divine life reorders our everyday exchanges. For embedded in the Eucharist is a "glimpse and foretaste of the ultimate good for God's creation, which is God himself" (Long, 2000, 235). This is the one resource that denies scarcity and rejects competition. At this table, all are satiated because after the Resurrection, there can be no shortage of Christ (thus, historical quests for Jesus remain misguided attempts to discover a scarce commodity, which cannot be discovered through these means because it is not scarce). Precisely because Christ is inexhaustible, language such as *consumption* assumes a different meaning. To consume a commodity is to be oriented toward a desire that is not finally satisfying. To have one's life defined by this kind of consumption is to be bound by what Tolstoy termed, "the gnawing agony of desire." It is to be bound by the fear that there may not be enough for all—so I must consume before it disappears. However, to consume Christ is to know a different kind of desire—a non-competitive desire where I can consume without fear that my eating causes your hunger

(Pickstock, 1998, 121–66). This is not to overlook the limits of competitive goods; it is to reorient them. My everyday exchanges are to be made intelligible by my consumption of Christ's own life, and so we pray, "Recalling his death, resurrection, and ascension, we offer you these gifts." Our gifts are to be reordered by this recalling.

What does this mean concretely? It does not provide us with a blueprint for a global economic system. It does not tell us which global economic system the church must support. If a theological ethic must do this, if it must teach us how to rule on a global basis, then our modest proposal will be dismissed as asocial. If Christian theology must address the social problem as defined by Ernst Troeltsch—"How can the Church harmonize with these main forces (State and Society) in such a way that together they will form a unity of civilization?"—then this act of memory, which the Eucharist is, will not be able to be viewed by theologians or ethicists as a viable "social ethic" (Troeltsch, 1981, 32). However, that may say more about what theologians and ethicists think about the nature of the church and God's relationship to it, than about social ethics. Our modest proposal is not a "social ethic" in terms of an application of social principles to something called "society" that will allow us to rule and order it. Far from such a social ethic, (if such exists other than in the minds and books of social ethicists), this modest proposal draws on concrete, everyday practices. And its purpose is to show how Christian persons might begin to think of their lives as oriented by Christ's offering for us rather than by the consumerist culture which receives its orientation from other concrete, everyday practices such as superhighways, malls, and food courts. To have our lives oriented by Christ is to become friends who consume in common, rather than individuals who consume in order to remain free from each other.

The logic of the contemporary market is not one of friendship and obligation. Instead, goods are alienated from the common life inasmuch as the only common life sustainable is the consumption of such goods. Goods are made possible by a relationship that presumes all exchanges are located in the disinterested will of the participating individuals. Such "disinterest" presupposes both sacrifice and alienation from such goods that, ironically, renders those goods nothing more than commodities, in that they are only defined by the subjective "commodious" character individuals attribute to them. Yet, gifts are neither commodities nor sacrificial acts. Gifts are marked by a social reciprocity that, within the church, finds its greatest intelligibility. Gifts cannot be alienated from the giver because the gift extends through time and space in the lives of those who receive them. Goods are only goods if they are for something that the community calls a good. Goods, in order to be a good, must be directed toward an end, and in the church, that end is friendship with God. All our goods, therefore, can only truly be good if they cultivate the habits and dispositions necessary to direct us toward this end.

# NOTES

1    For a fuller discussion of this see my, "Ecclesial Disobedience or Ecclesial Subordination to Liberal Institutions?" (Long, 2003).

2    This is to suggest that everything is theological, but not that "everything is political." The tendency for political theology to make everything political only serves to depoliticize theology. As Oliver O'Donovan wisely quips, "Political theology that follows this route often tends up paradoxically banishing politics as a theme of discussion, since every conceivable human enterprise, from biblical criticism to blowing our noses, is hailed as a 'political' gesture—meaning no more than it is undertaken in a self-assertive and anti-authoritarian spirit" (O'Donovan, 2005, 234). I concur with O'Donovan's sentiment here, and seek to address it below in chapter 3, "What Makes Theology 'Political'?" To say everything is political, and mean by that every claim to truth or goodness is in actuality a veiled claim to power is rampant in contemporary theology, but nevertheless silly.

3    Wheelan notes, "One can use the futures markets to mitigate risk—or one can use the futures market to bet on the price of soybeans next year." (Wheelan, 2002, 125).

4    "[Financial value is essentially a degree of hope, expectation or credibility . . . the value of money is essentially religious. To believe in the value of wealth is to believe in a promise that can never be realized; it is a religious faith. . . . Here ontology is mediated to practice on the basis of credit. . . . . The fundamental error [of Douglas claim that we replace "credit" with a "correlation between the production of money and the production of wealth"] is to invoke once more the naturalistic metaphysics of the 'real world,' overlooking the question of ontology, and the conditions of possibility of belief. And questions of ontology, politics and credit meet in the sphere of theology" (Goodchild, 2005, 135, 138).

5    Of course, we could easily dismiss this question with the all too familiar modern strategy of distinguishing a private from a public realm and cordoning off Jesus' teaching into some private realm of charitable giving. But we all know that private/public distinction only strengthens the intermediation of state politics and "networks of utility" over all our exchanges, leaving the church in the perilous state of therapeutic chaplain it finds itself within western secularist politics (even in their religious guise). Jesus does not fulfill the Law by retreating to some private place; he does it publicly before the watching world. He does so by raising the important metaphysical questions of credit and interest. In so doing he forever reminds us that these questions are not only economic but also theological and ethical (see Desmond, 2005, 165).

6    Ths same point was reaffirmed ten years later in the letter, "A Catholic Framework for Economic Life" where it states, "All economic life should be shaped by moral principles. Economic choices and institutions must be judged by how they protect or

undermine the life and dignity of the human person, support the family, and serve the comon good."

7 A proposed policy change is said to be, "Pareto superior" if it results in someone's being made better off without anyone's being made worse off. A situation in which it is impossible to make someone better off without making someone worse off is said to be, "Pareto efficient."

8 In 1996 Liggett admitted publicly that cigarettes are addictive. It settled several class-action lawsuits and is cooperating with the federal government's investigations of the tobacco industry.

9 For instance, take this rather universal and customary claim put forth by educators, "smaller classes tend to be a more effective way of teaching so let us have smaller class sizes." But economists recognize that smaller class sizes also increase expenses—limiting the socioeconomic status of students in those classes. Thus, both the benefits and the costs must be taken into consideration in determining optimal class size. It is this necessary reality check that has contributed to the unfortunate description of economics as "the dismal science."

10 See, e.g., Gary Becker and Richard Posner, both of the "Chicago School" of economics. For an indictment of their approach see Margaret Jane Radiin, *Contested Commodities: The Trouble with Trade in Sex, Children, Body Parts, and Other Things* (Cambridge, Mass.: Harvard University Press, 1996).

11 I must say a word here about the importance of the university as a place where this shared nervousness can be explored. This is not because of some sentimental idea of the university as an arena of free speech and neutral objectivity where truth is pursued dispassionately. Secular universities would not invite a Methodist theologian and a Jewish economist to expose their differences in disciplinary methodology and content. St. Joseph's University could invite us to teach this course precisely because it does not seek to instill a "neutral and objective" rationality

in its students. Without its Jesuit tradition, such an invitation would be difficult to fathom.

12 Even Long concedes that socialism has not succeeded in this regard and, in any case, has "lost" to capitalism.

13 In some countries, it is legal to buy one's way out of military service. The price is $16,000 in Iran (*New York Times Magazine*, 11/1/98, p. 55).

14 For example, see Joerg Rieger's, "Theology and Economics," *Religious Studies Review* 28 (2002): 216.

15 I recognize I am using a limited conception of a "theological work" in that I am assuming it is a published work. I am willing to consider other kinds of works as theological, but the debate I am referring to here is one that primarily takes place through published means.

16 The objection that not all social sciences are "Weberian" is certainly warranted. There may be examples of theologians who use the social sciences and do not fall prey to the kind of apodictic practical reasoning critiqued above.

17 That Niebuhr labels this "Augustinian realism" is, of course, quite ironic. After all, Augustine gave us this doctrine of the church. Niebuhr does recognize this, but also suggests that Augustine was inconsistent in describing the church as the "perfect society." Niebuhr offers many "reservations" about Augustine's position; nevertheless he calls it an "error." In fact, Niebuhr identifies another error in Augustine even graver than his identification of the visible church as a perfect society. He writes, "This error is probably related to the conception of grace which does not allow for the phenomenon, emphasized by the Reformation, that men may be redeemed in the sense that they consciously turn from self to Christ as their end, and yet they are not redeemed from the corruption of egotism which expresses itself, even in the lives of the saints. This insight is most succinctly expressed in Luther's phrase, 'Justus et peccator simul'" ("Augustine's Political Realism," in Niebuhr, 1977, 137–38).

18   *Federalist Papers*, 16.

19   *Federalist Papers*, 6.

20   I need to thank Dan Bell for his helpful comments on this essay.

21   The Dodge brothers brought this suit against Ford because they needed the dividends he then withheld so they could finance their own business enterprise.

22   Klassen writes, "Any thought of exacting usury was foreign to a movement that was characterized by a constant emphasis upon, and practice of, mutual aid."

23   Did this occur in Saudi Arabia in 1952 with the "royal decree" from the Saudi Arabian Monetary Agency that, as Buckley noted, may have issued the first "prohibition against interest" in an "official document" by a "Muslim country"? (Buckley, 2000, 278).

24   The Austrian school originated in Vienna with the work of Carl Menger (1840–1921). His contribution to economics was the development of the marginal theory of utility, which viewed exchange in terms of subjective preferences that could be ordered hierarchically. This led the Austrian school to emphasize consumption instead of the emphasis on production by the classical liberals. Menger's work was developed by Friedrich von Weiser (1851–1926) who developed the idea of opportunity costs and then by Eugene Böhm-Bawerk (1851–1941), Ludwig von Mises (1881–1973) and Friedrich von Hayek (1899-1995).

25   *De malo,* reply to 17: "It is one thing to consent or concur with someone in wickedness, another thing to use the wickedness of someone for good; for he consents or concurs with another in wickedness to whom it is pleasing that that other person engage in wickedness, and perhaps induces him to it, and this is always a sin; but he uses another's wickedness who turns this evil that someone does to some good, and in this way God uses the sins of men by eliciting from them some good; hence, it is lawful too for a man to use the sin of another for good. And this

is clear from Augustine who, when Publicola asked whether it was lawful to make use of an oath of a person swearing by false gods and obviously sinning in this, answered that he who uses, not for an evil but for a good purpose the sincerity of a man who certainly swore by false gods does not become a party to his sin of swearing by demons but to his honest contract by which he kept his word. However if it were pleasing to someone that another would swear by false gods and would induce him to it, he would sin."

26    Note that Calvin does offer seven qualifications on the practice of usury: 1. "No one should take interest from the poor"; 2. "Whoever loans should not be so preoccupied with gain as to neglect his necessary duties, nor wishing to protect his money, disdain his poor brothers"; 3. "No principle be followed that is not in accord with natural equity"; 4. "Whoever borrows should make at least as much, if not more than the amount borrowed"; 5. "We ought not to determine what is lawful by basing it on the common practice or in accordance with the iniquity of the world, but should base it on a principle derived from the word of God"; 6. "We should keep in mind what is best for the common good"; 7. "One ought not to exceed the rate that a country's public laws allow." And Calvin emphasizes that no one should have usury as "his form of occupation."

27    Langholm, 1992, 159. This is based on the biblical teaching that the worker is worthy of her or his wages. "He who works does not want," as Bonaventure writes. Langholm states, "This is a labour theory of sorts, although perhaps of a political rather than an economic nature, and hardly a labour theory of value."

28    Noonan writes, "Cajetan was a man of enormous ability, prestige and power. . . . Considered by many to have been the ablest Thomistic philosopher since Saint Thomas, he treats of economic morals with the astuteness, care and subtlety that distinguished him in metaphysics. Not infected by Conrad's basic skepticism towards the usury rule, he is a loyal Thomist here as

elsewhere. But, as Saint Thomas adapted Aristotle, so he adapts Saint Thomas, and his own views, large and liberal for his age, use the original Thomistic teaching only as a starting point" (Noonan, 1957, 211). Cajetan's defense of the triple contract is a sign of a mature economics that accommodates the inevitable. Henri de Lubac found Cajetan a less than faithful interpreter of Aquinas because he taught that the human person had both a natural and supernatural end and these were not integrated. This allowed moral and political theology to be developed, supposedly in Thomistic terms, without reference to Christ. De Lubac gives us a better account of nature and grace in Thomistic moral theology, which David Schindler characterizes as "organic" and "paradoxical." It is organic because "nature is created with a single final end, which is supernatural, that relation to this end (to the God of Jesus Christ) therefore orients nature from the beginning of natural existence." However, it is also paradoxical in that this single end does not "neglect the radical distinction between nature and grace—to the neglect of the utter gratuity and novelty introduced by grace (hence the term paradox)" (Schindler, 1996, 52 n. 12).

29   Joan Lockwood O'Donovan noted that one of the significant contributions Odd Langholm makes in his analysis of medieval economics is his challenge to "the dismissive assessment of usury theory within his discipline." However she also notes that Langholm's work is "ambiguous" toward the scholastic analysis, finding in it both continuity with modern economics critical of the classical tradition and discontinuity between modern "theoretical foundations" and ancient Aristotelian moral rationality. The result is a lack of adequate attention to the theological foundations of the usury prohibition. O'Donovan, "The Theological Economics of Medieval Usury Theory" in O'Donovan et al., 2004, 97.

30   "And so it comes about that working men are now left isolated and helpless, betrayed to the inhumanity of employers and the

unbridled greed of competitors. Voracious usury makes matters worse, an evil condemned frequently by the church but nevertheless still practiced in deceptive ways by avaricious men" (Leo XIII, *Rerum Novarum*, para. 2 in Walsh, *Proclaiming Justice and Peace*, 17).

31    "Schumpeter's view of economic analysis seems to be wholly compatible with the position of the papal encyclical on the 'Restoration of the Social Order'" (Dempsey, 1958, 12).

32    See the *The Functional Economy*, where he argued that "natural truths and logical reasoning" alone form the basis for economic analysis (65). Likewise, in his *Interest and Usury*, he argued that the medievals did their analysis solely based on "facts" to determine what is "right and just" (1).

33    *De malo* 1.2. resp.

34    *De malo* 1.1: "Just as the color white is spoken of in two ways, so also is evil. For in one way when white is said, it can refer to that which is the subject of whiteness, in another way to the whiteness itself, namely the accident or quality itself. And likewise when evil is said, it can refer to that which is the subject of evil, and this is something; in another way, it can refer to the evil itself, and this is not something but is the privation of some particular good."

35    *De malo* 13.1 obj. 7: "No special sin is contrary to diverse virtues because one thing is contrary to one thing, as is said in Book X of the *Metaphysics*. But avarice is contrary to diverse virtues: for it is contrary to charity, as Augustine says; it is also contrary to liberality as is commonly said; it is also contrary to justice inasmuch as justice is a special virtue, as Chrysostom says in explaining *Matthew* (5, 6) 'Blessed are they who hunger and thirst for righteousness'; for righteousness signifies either a general virtue or a particular virtue opposed to avarice. Therefore avarice is not a special sin."

36    See Fukuyama, 1992; Vattimo, 1988; Bell, 2001); and Schumpeter, 1975, 123–24.

37    For a helpful discussion on how the modern corporation is forced into this kind of behavior, see Mitchell, 2001. Mitchell argues that the artificial nature of the corporation as an individual within the context of American liberalism, coupled with limited liability and the moral imperative to maximize profit, leads to "corporate irresponsibility." He offers a number of examples of such irresponsibility in modern corporations, including Firestone, Ford, Hooker Chemical, Union Carbide, General Electric, Mattel, Coca-Cola, Unocal, General Motors, and Marriot Corporation (19–49).

38    Gutiérrez, 1993, 22–23. But see also p. 157 where Gutiérrez recognizes that even Catholic social teaching reads conflict as a "social fact."

39    For an excellent critique of the doctrine of Christian vocation as a form of theological legitimation for business activity, see Robert Brimlow, *Paganism and the Professions*. Brimlow gives a much more realistic assessment of what work is, and requires of us, than most of the romantic appeals to the notion of vocation one finds in church documents and in theological writings. As Brimlow notes, "It is hard to maintain that, for the vast majority of us, work is intrinsically good. For most of us, work is instrumental; it is the means by which we can pursue other ends: feeding and housing ourselves and our loved ones and purchasing things that make life more comfortable. It is rare to find people who work at jobs where they find any but the most minimal types of fulfillment or where they recognize that their work satisfies a higher purpose other than increased profitability for the firm." (6).

40    They write, "Enhancing the capacity for capitalization in responsible corporations is as much the new name for mission as development is the new name for peace" (Stackhouse and McCann, 1995, 952).

41    In *After Virtue*, MacIntyre refuses to concede that at the end of modernity liberalism and Marxism do not represent two

contrasting positions; they are not an either/or because, as he puts it, "the claim of Marxism to a morally distinctive standpoint is undermined by Marxism's own moral history. . . . Marxists have always fallen back into relatively straightforward versions of Kantianism or utilitarianism. This is not surprising. Secreted within Marxism from the outset, is a certain radical individualism. . . . Secondly, I remarked earlier that as Marxists move towards power they always tend to become Weberians" (1984, 261). Milbank also finds Marx remains "an economic thinker" within the liberal tradition in that he does not "fully recognize the historical particularity of the economic." It is distinguished from other forms of exchange, like religious exchange, and valued as their real meaning. Moreover, as Milbank notes, Marx failed to recognize that "it is just as fundamental for capitalist logic to reproduce conditions of exchange and consumption as to reproduce the conditions of production." Thus, the labor theory of value alone cannot account for the value attributed to produce goods. See Milbank, 1990, 191.

42  It is Kant's "third antinomy" (which has other precursors in the philosophical tradition) that makes this kind of division of intellectual labor possible. And once we adopt the "linguistic turn" (Hamann-Herder-Humboldt in continental philosophy or Frege-Wittgenstein in the English tradition), this kind of division can no longer be safely assumed. No "social fact" exists without its narratabililty through language.

43  I am not presuming that there are only these two theological languages. I am only arguing that these two represent the dominant languages most theologians explicitly or implicitly adopt.

# SELECT BIBLIOGRAPHY

Alison, James. 1996. *Raising Abel*. New York: Crossroad-Herder.

Anderson, Elizabeth. 1990. "The Ethical Limitations of the Market." *Economics and Philosophy* 6: 179–205.

———. 1993. *Value in Ethics and Economics*. Cambridge, Mass.: Harvard University Press.

Aquinas, Thomas. 1993. *On Evil*. Translated by Jean Oesterle. Notre Dame, Ind.: University of Notre Dame Press.

———. 1948. *Summa Theologia*. Translated by Fathers of the English Dominican Province. Westminster, Md.: Christian Classics.

Bandow, Doug, and Wendel Novak. 2003. *Poverty and Human Destiny*. Wilmington Del.: ISI Books

Bandow, Doug, and David Schindler, eds. 2003. *Wealth, Poverty and Human Destiny*. Wilmington, Del.: ISI Books.

Baumol, William, and Alan Blinder. 1991. *Economics, Principles and Policy*. 5th ed. San Diego: Harcourt Brace Jovanovich.

———. 1997. *Microeconomics: Principles and Policy*. 7th ed. Fort Worth: The Dryden Press.

Bell, Daniel M., Jr. 2001. *Liberation Theology after the End of History.* London: Routledge.

Benthan, Jeremy. 1952. Letter XIII, "Defence of Usury." In Jeremy Bentham's *Economic Writings.* Edited by W. Stark. London: Black-friars.

Berry, Wendell. 1991. "The Mad Farmer Liberation Front." In *Context: A Quarterly of Humane Sustainable Culture* (Fall/Winter).

Blank, Rebecca M., and William McGurn. 2004. *Is the Market Moral?* Washington D.C.: Brookings.

Blinder, Alan S. 1987. *Hard Heads, Soft Hearts: Tough Minded Economics for a Just Society.* Reading, Mass.: Addison Wesley.

Böhm-Bawerk, Eugen von. 1959. *Capital and Interest.* Translated by George D. Huncke and Hans F. Sennholz. South Holland, Ill.: Libertarian, 1959.

Borgmann, Albert. 1987. *Technology and the Character of Contemporary Life.* Chicago: University of Chicago Press.

Boulton, Wayne, G., Thomas D. Kennedy, and Allen Verhey, eds. 1994. *From Christ to the World.* Grand Rapids: Eerdmans.

Brimlow, Robert. 2001. *Paganism and the Professions.* Ekklesia Project Pamphlet Series, no. 3. Eugene, Ore.: Wipf & Stock.

Brue, Stanley. 1994. *The Evolution of Economic Thought.* Fort Worth: The Dryden Press.

Buckley, Susan. 2000. *Teachings on Usury in Judaism, Christianity and Islam.* Lewiston, N.Y.: The Edwin Mellen Press.

Byasse, Jason. 2005. "The New Monasticism." *The Christian Century* (September): 38–47.

Cavanaugh, William. 1999. "The Eucharist as Resistance to Globalization." *Modern Theology* 15.2.

Colander, David C. 1991. *Why Aren't Economists as Important as Garbagmen: Essays on the State of Economics.* New York: M. E. Sharpe.

Cooley, Charles H. 1913. "The Institutional Character of Pecuniary Valuation." *The American Journal of Sociology* 18.4: 543–55.

Davies, Brian, and Michael Walsh. 1991. *Proclaiming Justice and Peace.* San Fransisco: Harper Collins.

Dempsey, Bernard. 1958. *The Functional Economy*. Englewood Cliffs, N.J.: Prentice Hall.

———. 1943. *Interest and Usury*. Washington, D.C.: American Council on Public Affairs.

Derrida, Jacques. 1995. *The Gift of Death*. Translated by David Wills. Chicago: University of Chicago Press.

Desmond, William. 2005. "Neither Servility nor Sovereignty: Between Metaphysics and Politics." In *Theology and the Political: The New Debate*. Edited by Creston Davis, John Milbank, and Slavoj Zizek. Durham, N.C.: Duke University Press.

Dorrien, Gary J. 2004. *Imperial Designs: Neoconservatism and the New Pax Americana*. New York: Routledge.

Duffy, Eamon. 1992. *The Stripping of the Altars: Traditional Religion in England 1400–1580*. New Haven: Yale University Press.

Frank, Robert. 1998. *Principles of Microeconomics*. San Francisco: McGraw-Hill.

Friedman, Milton. 2006. "The Social Responsibility oof Business is to Increase its Profits." In *Taking Sides*. Edited by Frank J. Bortello. Dubuque, Iowa: McGraw-Hill/Duskin. 4–9.

Fleischacker, Samuel. 2004. *On Adam Smith's Wealth of Nations: A Philosophical Companion*. Princeton: Princeton University Press.

Fukuyama, Francis. 1992. *The End of History and the Last Man*. New York: The Free Press.

Galbraith, John Kenneth. 1976. *The Affluent Society*. New York: New American Library.

Goodchild, Philip. 2005. "Capital and Kingdom: An Eschatological Ontology." In *Theology and the Political: The New Debate*. Edited by Creston Davis, John Milbank, and Slavoj Zizek. Durham, N.C.: Duke University Press.

Griffiths, Paul, and Reinhard Hütter. 2005. *Reason and the Reasons of Faith*. London: Continuum.

Gutiérrez, Gustavo. 1993. A Theology of Liberation. Maryknoll, N.Y.: Orbis Press.

Hayek, F. A. 1994. *The Road to Serfdom.* Chicago: University of Chicago Press.

Heilbronner, Robert. 1986. *The Worldly Philosophers: The Lives, Times and Ideas of the Great Economic Thinkers.* New York: Simon & Schuster.

Hirshleifer, Jack, and Amihai Glazer. 1992. *Price Theory and Applications.* 5th ed. Englewood Cliffs, N.J.: Prentice Hall.

Hobbes, Thomas. 1983. *Leviathan.* Glasgow: Collins & Fount Paperbacks. Originally published in 1651.

Hubmaier, Balthasar. 1993. *The Lord's Supper in Anabaptism: A Study in the Christology of Balthasar Hubmaier, Pilgram Marpeck, and Dirk Philips.* Waterloo: Herald Press.

Jevons, William Stanley. 1888. *The Theory of Political Economy.* 3rd ed. London: Macmillan.

Jones, David. 2004. *Reforming the Morality of Usury.* Lanham, M.D.: University Press of America.

Katz, Michale L., and Harvey S. Rosen. 1991. *Microeconomics.* Homewood, Ill.: Richard D. Irwin.

Kaufman, Walter, ed. 1983. *The Portable Nietzsche.* London: Penguin Books.

Keynes, John Maynard. 1964. *General Theory Of Employment, Interest and Money.* San Diego: Harcourt Brace.

Kierkegaard, Søren. 1995. *Works of Love.* Translated by Howard V. Hong and Edna H. Hong. Princeton: Princeton University Press.

Klassen, Peter. 1964. *The Economics of Anabaptism.* London: Mouton & Co.

Knight, Frank. 1969. "Ethics and the Economic Interpretation." In *The Ethics of Competition and Other Essays.* Freeport, N.Y.: Books for Libraries Press, 1969.

Langholm, Odd. 1992. *Economics in the Medieval Schools.* Leiden: E. J. Brill.

Leo XIII. 1994. Rerum Novarum. In *Proclaiming Justice and Peace.* Edited by Michael Walsh and Brian Davies. Mystic, Conn.: Twenty-Third Publications.

Leonard, John. 2002. "Did Milton Go to the Devil's Party." *New York Review of Books* 49.12.

Liebenstein, Harvey. 1948. "Bandwagon, Snob, and Veblen Effects in the Theory of Consumers' Demand." *Quarterly Journal of Economics* 62: 165–201.

Long, D. Stephen. 2000. *Divine Economy: Theology and the Market.* London: Routledge.

———. 2003. "Ecclesial Disobedience or Ecclesial Subordination to Liberal Institutions?" In *Staying the Course: Supporting the Church's Position on Homosexuality.* Edited by Maxie E. Dunnam and H. Newton Maloney. Nashville: Abingdon.

MacIntyre, Alasdair. 1984. *After Virtue.* Notre Dame, Ind.: University of Notre Dame Press..

———. 1995. *First Principles, Final Ends and Contemporary Philosophical Issues.* Milwaukee, Wisc.: Marquette University Press.

———. 1994. "How Can We Learn What *Veritatis Splendor* Has To Teach." *The Thomist* 58 (1994): 171–95.

———. 1995. "Introduction 1953, 1968, 1995: Three Perspectives." *Marxism and Christianity.* Notre Dame, Ind.: University of Notre Dame Press.

———. 1988. *Whose Justice? Which Rationality?* Notre Dame, Ind.: University of Notre Dame Press.

Mansnerus, Laura. 1998. "Market Puts Price Tags on the Priceless." *The New York Times*, October 26, p. 1.

Marshall, Alfred. 1925a. "Mr. Mills' Theory of Value (1876)." In *Memorials of Alfred Marshall.* Edited by A. C. Pigou. London: Macmillan.

———. 1925b. "The Present Position of Economics (1885)." In *Memorials of Alfred Marshall.* Edited by A. C. Pigou. London: Macmillan.

———. 1920. *Principles of Economics.* 8th ed. London: Macmillan. Originally published 1890.

Mauss, Marcel. 1990. *The Gift: The Form and Reason for Exchange in Archaic Societies.* Translated W. D. Halls. London: Routledge.

McCarthy, David Matzko. 2001. *Sex and Love in the Home*. London: SCM Press.

Menger, Carl. 1950. *Principles of Economics*. Translated and edited James Dingwall and Bert F. Hoselitz. Glencoe, Ill.: Free Press.

Milbank, John. 1986. "The Body by Love Possessed: Christianity and Late Capitalism in Britain." *Modern Theology* 3.1: 35–65.

———. 1995. "Can a Gift Be Given? Prolegomena to a Future Trinitarian Metaphysic." *Modern Theology* 21.1: 119–61.

———. 1992. "Enclaves, or Where is the Church?" *New Blackfriars* 73.801: 341–52.

———. 1996. "Socialism of the Gift, Socialism by Grace." *New Blackfriars* 77.910: 532–48.

———. 1990. *Theology and Social Theory*. Oxford: Basil Blackwell.

———. 1997. *The Word Made Strange*. Oxford: Blackwell.

Mill, J. S. 1975. *On Liberty*. New York: W.W. Norton.

Mitchell, Lawrence. 2001. *Corporate Irresponsibility: America's Newest Export*. New Haven: Yale University Press, 2001.

Nelson, Benjamin. 1969. The Idea of Usury: From Tribal Brotherhood to Universal Otherhood. Chicago: University of Chicago Press.

Niebuhr, Reinhold. 1977. *Christian Realism and Political Problems*. Fairfield, N.J.: A. M. Kelley, rpt.; originally published in 1953.

———. 1963. *An Interpretation of Christian Ethics*. San Francisco: Harper & Row.

Nietzsche, Friedrich. 1983. *The Portable Nietzsche*. Translated by Walter Kaufmann. New York: Penguin Books.

Noonan, John T. Jr. 1957. *The Scholastic Analysis of Usury*. Cambridge, Mass.: Harvard University Press.

Novak, Michael. 1993. *The Catholic Ethic and the Spirit of Capitalism*. New York: The Free Press.

———. 1999a. "Controversial Engagements." *First Things* 92: 21–29. http://www.first.things.com/article.php3?id-article=3136.

———. 1999b. "How Christianity Created Capitalism." *Wall Street Journal*, December 23, A18.

———. 1995. "Toward a Theology of the Corporation." In Stackhouse et al.

———. 1982. *The Spirit of Democratic Capitalism*. New York: American Enterprise Institute/Simon & Schuster.

O'Donovan, Joan Lockwood, and Oliver O'Donovan. 2005. *The Bonds of Imperfection*. Grand Rapids: Eerdmans.

Okun, Arthur. 1975. *Equality and Efficiency: The Big Tradeoff*. Washington, D.C.: The Brookings Institution.

Palmiter, Robert. 2004. *Corporations: Examples & Explanations*. 4th ed. New York: Aspen Publishers.

Pickstock, Catherine. 1998. *After Writing: The Liturgical Consummation of Philosophy*. Oxford: Blackwell.

Radin, Margaret Jane. 1996. *Contested Commodities: The Trouble with Trade in Sex, Children, Body Parts and Other Things*. Cambridge, Mass.: Harvard University Press.

Ratzinger, Joseph Cardinal. 2003. *Truth and Tolerance: Christian Belief and World Religions*. San Francisco: Ignatius Press.

Rempel, John. 1993. *The Lord's Supper in Anabaptism*. Waterloo, Ontario: The Herald Press.

Rieger, Joerg. 2001. *God and the Excluded*. Minneapolis: Fortress.

———. 2002. "Theology and Economics." *Religious Studies Review* 28: 216.

Rose-Ackerman, Susan. 1998. "Inalienability." In *The New Palgrave Dictionary of Economics and the Law*. Edited by Peter Newman. New York: Stockton Press. 268–73.

Schindler, David. 1996. *Heart of the World, Center of the Church: "Communio Ecclesiology, Liberalism and Liberation."* Grand Rapids: Eerdmans.

Schumpeter, Joseph A. 1975. *Capitalism, Socialism and Democracy*. New York: Harper Torchbooks.

Skidelsky, Robert. 1994. *John Maynard Keynes: The Economist as Savior, 1920-1937*. London: Penguin Books.

Smith, Adam. 1877. *An Inquiry into the Nature and Causes of the Wealth of Nations.* New York: G. P. Putnam's Sons. Originally published in 1776.

———. 1965. *The Wealth of Nations.* New York: The Modern Library/ Random House.

———. 1982. *The Theory of Moral Sentiments.* Indianapolis: Liberty Fund.

Smith, James K. 2004. *Introducing Radical Orthodoxy.* Grand Rapids: Baker Academic.

Stackhouse, Max, Dennis P. McCann, and Shirley J. Roels, with Preston N. Williams, eds. 1995. *On Moral Business.* Grand Rapids: Eerdmans.

Tamari, Meir. 1991. *In the Marketplace: Jewish Business Ethics.* Southfield, Mich.: Targum Press.

Tanner, Kathryn. 2005. *Economy of Grace.* Minneapolis: Fortress.

———. 2004. "In Praise of Open Communion: A Rejoinder to James Farwell." *Anglican Theological Review* (Summer): 473–85.

———. 2001. *Jesus, Humanity and the Trinity.* Minneapolis: Fortress.

Tawney, R. H. 1954. *Religion and the Rise of Capitalism.* New York: Mentor Book.

Taylor, Charles. 1995. *Philosophical Arguments.* Cambridge, Mass.: Harvard University Press.

Toffler, Barbara Ley. 2003. *Final Accounting: Ambition, Greed and the Fall of Arthur Andersen.* New York: Doubleday.

Troeltsch, Ernest. 1981. *The Social Teaching of the Christian Churches.* Vol. 1 and 2. Translated by Olive Wyon. Chicago: University of Chicago Press.

Vattimo, Gianni. 1988. *The End of Modernity.* Baltimore: The Johns Hopkins University Press.

Veblen, Thorstein. 1934. *The Leisure Class.* New York: The Modern Library.

Von Balthasar, Hans Urs. 1994. *Theo-Drama Theological Dramatic Theory.* Vol. IV: *The Action.* Translated by Graham Harrison. San Francisco: Ignatius Press.

Waldfogel, Joel. 1998. "The Deadweight Loss of Christmas." *The American Economic Review* 83.5: 1328–36.

Weatherford, Jack. 1998. *The History of Money.* New York: Three Rivers Press.

Weber, Max. 1978. *Economy and Society.* Vol. 1. Edited by Guenther Roth and Claus Wittich. Berkeley: University of California Press..

———. 1958. *From Max Weber: Essays in Sociology.* Edited and translated by H. H. Gerth and C. Wright Mills. New York: Oxford University Press.

Weindandy, Thomas G. 2000. *Does God Suffer?* Notre Dame, Ind.: University of Notre Dame Press.

Wheelan, Charles. 2002. *Naked Economics: Undressing the Dismal Science.* New York: W.W. Norton.

Wilkin, John, ed. 1999. *Considering Veritatis Splendor.* Cleveland, Ohio: The Pilgim Press.

Williams, Rowan. 1999. *On Christian Theology.* London: Blackwell.

———. 2000. *Lost Icons: Reflections on Cultural Bereavement.* Edinburgh: T&T Clark.

Yoder, John Howard. 1994. *Body Politics.* Nashville: Abingdon.

———. 2003. *The Jewish-Christian Schism Revisited.* Edited by Michael G. Cartwright and Peter Ochs. Grand Rapids: Eerdmans.

Zelizer, Viviana A. 1996. *The Social Meaning of Money.* New York: Basic Books.

Zizek, Slavoj. 2000. *The Fragile Absolute—or why the Christian legacy is worth fighting for?* London: Verso.

# INDEX